get a
cosmic
clue

astrology, numerology, fengshui,
andotherhelpfromtheheavens

get a
cosmic
clue

astrology, numerology, fengshui, and other help from the heavens

by Lori Stacy

Scholastic Inc.

New York • Toronto • London • Auckland • Sydney
Mexico City • New Delhi • Hong Kong • Buenos Aires

Interior Illustrations: Lisa Parett
Design: Mark Neston

ISBN 0-439-27221-1

12 11 10 9 8 7 6 5 4 3 2   4 5 6/0
Printed in the U.S.A.
First Scholastic printing, July 2001

Table
of Contents

Intro

Let's face it—there are a lot of hard-to-answer questions in life. Like why does your crush seem totally into you one day, then act as if you don't exist the next? Or why do you come unglued when you can't have things your way? Or even why is it that you can't seem to bond with one particular friend? Nobody has all the answers, but maybe, just maybe, astrology can answer a few of them!

Astrology is ages-old, and yet it continues to be practiced by people of all different ages and all different cultures. And things like numerology and Feng Shui are also starting to infiltrate our culture as well. You just gotta believe that there's something to all of this—that the heavens and the earth have an effect on people's moods and personalities. And that while your environment and other unique-to-you influences certainly shape who you are, there are some things you're just born with.

The pages of this book include insight into who you are based on some of these ancient astrological principles. You'll come across things that you're well aware of in yourself, and find out a few new personality quirks that can help explain your behavior better. You can also read up on the traits of your friends, family members, and boyfriends to try to get a better understanding of them. We may not have all the answers here, but no doubt the info will provide some insight into the story of you!

Part One

'Scoping Things Out

Ever wonder how and why your astrological sign can say so much about you? Well, here's the deal: Ancient astronomers made the connection that what was happening with the sun, the moon, and the planets had an effect on what was happening on earth. They determined that planetary influences at the time of a person's birth helped shape who that person would be, and based the signs of the zodiac on the sun's movement into one of twelve constellations every thirty days. And boy, were they right!

Your sign can give a pretty accurate overview of who you are, why you do the things you do, and why you click with some people and collide with others. The signs are also associated with certain colors, flowers, and gemstones—all of which can create a more positive vibe with people born under those signs.

And there's more to astrology than just your ruling sign. Charting things out using your exact time of birth can give you even more clues about your unique personality. (Which is why that girl you know who has the same sign as you is not your personality double.) Your sign alone can shed some major light on your life and help tell you what you're all about.

Need more convincing? Read on for a few cosmic clues about you!

aquarius

(January 20 to February 18)

aquarius fast facts

Symbol: The Water Bearer

Element: Air

Ruling Planet: Uranus

Color: Insightful indigo blue

Flower: Hyacinth

Gemstone: Amethyst

Day: Saturday

the aquarius girl

Aquarius girls dance to the beat of their own drums. They are the most unique and original sign, and their behavior can sometimes be construed as eccentric. You prefer to work outside the system—if everyone is doing a written presentation for history class, you'll opt for an oral exam. To you, the status quo is meant to be messed with. The Water Bearer is also a visionary—you've got big dreams and they are anything but ordinary. Because you've been on the receiving end of misjudgments about your character, you find it easy to accept other people's differences. You probably have a wide circle of friends from all different backgrounds. Rebellion is also part of an Aquarius girl's nature. Those who try to make you behave a certain way will quickly learn that an Aquarian needs to exercise her independence.

aquarius stellar traits

Strengths: You're original and independent.

Strikes: You sometimes pick fights just because you love to argue.

Loves: Making the world a better place

Loathes: Following rules

Looks: You could be a cast member on *That '70s Show*.

Hangout spot: A political rally

Soul mate: A guy who can make you laugh and shares your passion for justice

Friend trends: You choose friends who share your easygoing, non-judgmental attitude.

Movie match: *Austin Powers*

Celebs who share your sign: Jennifer Aniston, Nick Carter, Minnie Driver, Heather Graham, Seth Green, Michael Jordan, Justin Timberlake

deep thoughts

It's easy to mistake a rebel like you as a bad girl, but anyone who thinks that is wrong! You care an incredible amount about others and have a deep-seated need to try and save the world. It upsets you immensely to see someone sad or hurt, and you have a tendency to always root for the underdog. While your heart bleeds for others, you have a tough time getting in touch with your own feelings. Part of the reason is that you're so busy trying to save the world, that you forget to take time out for yourself. Don't take off when the topic of convo with your friends turns to you—open up and let them in!

your social side

Aquarius girls have the potential to be brainiacs—your way of taking things apart mentally helps you get to the top of the class. You also like to tinker with things—you not only mentally disassemble things, you physically take 'em apart, too. Mental games are your specialty. No, not head games—games that use your smarts, like board games or anything computer related. (So, how long ago was it that you created your own Web page, anyway?) Like the father of all brainiacs—Einstein—your mental capacity can create a few, shall we say, eccentricities in the Aquarius girl's personality.

Friends who understand your quirky side and think it's pretty cool are on the Aquarius keeper list. Ditto for girls who can bring out your offbeat side with equally offbeat comments. And OK, ditto for just about anyone—let's face it, Aquarians get along with almost everyone.

Aquarians also place a huge value on their friendships, so your buds had better be flake-free (uh, Pisces…that can be you at times). You'll quickly connect with an Aries, Gemini, or Libra girl. The balance you'll bring to a friendship with a Virgo or Scorpio will make you both better people…not that you needed much help, though!

Friendly signs for Aquarius: Aries, Gemini, Virgo, Libra, Scorpio, Capricorn

star style

Aquarius girls have a style that's all their own. You're a fashionista who goes out of her way to find the most unique and quirky clothes. As such, you spend a lot of time shopping or searching fashion mags for your next purchase. You aren't afraid to road test a trend that hasn't quite hit your hometown yet. Some are winners, while others earn you the "What was she thinking?" award. Who cares, though? To you, fashion should be fun. But while you want a look that's one-of-a-kind, you're also easily influenced by your style idols—models and actresses who you feel set the trends. (Were you not the first in line at your stylist's to get the Jennifer Aniston 'do?)

aquarius style sheet

Your best beauty feature: Your killer smile

Look you'll love: An armful of chunky bracelets

Wouldn't be caught dead in: Clothes that are boring or unimaginative—for you, the quirkier the better

Makeup item you can't live without: Clear lip gloss

Scent pick: Spicy, herbal scents with undertones of ginger or musk

Fashion diva: Jennifer Aniston

matters of the heart

Guys are initially attracted to an Aquarius girl by her open, friendly personality and the way she is a people magnet. But just wait 'til they get to know the real you—the side that's purposely kept from public view. They'll find a girl who's good to the core. Your generosity is revealed in relationships, and the lucky guy who nabs an Aquarius will be almost overwhelmed with thoughtful gestures. Kind and caring as you are, there's one sure way a guy can earn himself his walking papers: Since your independent streak can leave you wary of authority, guys who are controlling will push you away. A Capricorn guy can give you just the amount of space you need, so long as you don't read it as his being distant. There'll be no distance at all with a Virgo or a Gemini guy, even though the intensity could cause its share of arguments. Footloose Leos and Aries types will provide a laugh a minute and rarely a dull moment. However, the occasional gloom of the Taurus, Cancer, or Pisces can bring you down. With another Aquarius, get ready for some outrageous times and a dating life that's anything but ordinary.

the aquarius guy

It seems as though all of your friends have a huge crush on the same Aquarius guy you've got your eyes on. This guy is friendly to everyone. Combine that with a gorgeous bod and a great smile, and you've got the school's most eligible babe. So how will you win over this cutie? By being yourself. An Aquarius guy can spot a fake a mile away and is soooo turned off by anyone who's not genuine. It's much easier to start a relationship with an Aquarian as a friend, as he'll want to get to know you before he makes his move.

The Aquarius guy is also a true individual who can sometimes come across as eccentric and weird. He may not hang with the most normal group of guys, either. It's totally important to him that you understand what he's about and give him the space he needs to be himself.

aquarius guy file

Where to spot him: At a protest rally

Win his heart by: Being independent and unique

Great date: Volunteering at a local charity

Major annoyance: People who are unimaginative

Astro matches: Gemini, Aries, Libra

Aquarius hottie: Justin Timberlake

pisces

(February 19 to March 20)

pisces fast facts

Symbol: The Fish

Element: Water

Ruling Planet: Neptune

Color: Tame turquoise

Flower: Peony

Gemstone: Aquamarine

Day: Thursday

the pisces girl

Got a problem? Dial a Pisces. The most compassionate and sensitive sign in the zodiac, the Fish is always ready to lend a shoulder to a friend in need. (Heck, you'd lend a shoulder to a total stranger if you sensed she had a problem.) You can sometimes come across as shy because you are confident enough not to have to take center stage in a situation. You'll sit back and wait until someone starts a conversation with you. But when that person does get a convo going with you, she'll experience both sweetness and an offbeat sense of humor. Because you're more mellow than most, you have a tendency to be late to everything. Not much can get you to step on the gas and hurry up. You rarely make the first move socially, so pals of Pisces need to be the ones to plan the fun.

pisces stellar traits

Strengths: You're gentle and kind.

Strikes: You're *always* late.

Loves: Daydreaming

Loathes: Being rushed

Looks: Frilly and feminine

Hangout spot: Your backyard hammock

Soul mate: A sensitive type who'll write you love letters

Friend trends: You tend to take on your friends' probs—try for a little distance.

Movie match: *Shakespeare in Love*

Celebs who share your sign: Drew Barrymore, Jessica Biel, Thora Birch, Jennifer Love Hewitt, Brian Littrell, Freddie Prinze Jr., James Van Der Beek

deep thoughts

The girl who is most likely to take on all of her friends' troubles can often find herself stressing about problems that aren't even hers. (Here's a tip: Try to detach yourself from issues that are not only out of your life, but out of your control.) Because you seem to be a magnet for friends in need, it is essential that you have time to yourself. Chilling in your room to a new CD is your idea of a good time. Pisces will rush to help someone else, but you seem to not be in a big hurry otherwise. When you're given a school assignment, you tend to sit on things until the last possible moment. Then, just before it's due, you crack the books and study with a vengeance.

your social side

When it comes to finding a terrific team player, you need not look any farther than a Pisces girl. You're the type who'll show up at every practice and bring water for the rest of the team when it's sweltering outside. You don't need to have a star position on a team, and your altruistic ways make you the perfect defensive player. Why are you such the sports martyr? Simple—you are practically incapable of letting people down, and where better to show it than on the field or on the court.

Your intuitive abilities help you achieve good grades. Though you may be utterly perplexed by all those rules of grammar, your ability to grasp the meaning of things will let you ace English exams anyway. A Pisces's instincts will rarely steer her wrong. (Yet another reason you're so good at understanding other people's problems.)

You put those instincts to work when it comes to finding friends to bond with. Your crew is made up of girls with strong character and sweet souls. Sure, you have this uncanny ability to help anyone get through a crisis, but that doesn't mean that you're a magnet for people with problems. Instead, you want friends you can admire (something you do quite well). A warm-hearted Cancer, a deep and soulful Scorpio, or a rock-solid Aries makes a Pisces pal proud. The steadfast Taurus girl has also got qualities that you respect, and you'll be happy to help a Leo girl rise to any occasion. When you want to hit the party scene, your Sag friend will make it too fun to resist, while you may have a hard time dealing with a Capricorn's unbendable behavior. (You, Pisces girl, get a rush out of things done on the spur of the moment.)

Friendly signs for Pisces: Aries, Taurus, Cancer, Leo, Virgo, Scorpio

star style

When it comes to clothes, you're a definite girly-girl. You like looks that are ultra-feminine and go for romantic touches like embroidery, sequins, and shimmer—so long as it's not overdone. If anyone can go glam, it's a Pisces girl. While your day clothes may not put you on the school's best-dressed list, your night styles rock. If there's one look that seems to be a Pisces signature style, it's a peekaboo top or sweater that shows off a camisole underneath. Water sign that you are, you gravitate toward blues, greens, and other complementary colors like lilac and even pink. Your delicate accessories add shine to outfits, and your closet full of shoes is the envy of your friends.

pisces style sheet

Your best beauty feature: Your smooth shoulders

Look you'll love: A delicately embroidered sweater in a soft pastel

Wouldn't be caught dead in: Anything too tailored or conservative—you prefer feminine looks

Makeup item you can't live without: Pearlescent eye shadow

Scent pick: A light scent with undertones of exotic flowers

Fashion diva: Jennifer Love Hewitt

matters of the heart

There's nothing fishy about a Pisces girl in a relationship—you love to love and want a soul mate who'll be as into serious snuggling as you are. You'll notice things about a guy no girl has ever discovered, like how soft his lips are or how mesmerizing his eyes are. And you won't be afraid to tell him about it! Can he take such sweet musings? If he's also a water sign, like a Cancer, Scorpio, or another Pisces, chances are he'll be way into it. But practicality will not be a big part of a relationship with one of the water ones. In fact, you'll probably both blow through your cash before the week is over going out for a bite to eat together, again and again. A well-grounded Capricorn could introduce a little level-headedness into your world, while you introduce some passion into his. Because you are so into commitment, guys of the Aries, Aquarius, or Leo persuasion who value their freedom will drive you outta your mind. A Virgo or Sagittarius guy will be all over your TLC, but will they give you enough in return? Only time will tell with those two.

the pisces guy

Oh, to be the girl on the receiving end of a Piscean's romantic ways! If you can handle a sensitive guy (and not every girl can), you are in for some serious doting. He'll take you on the most romantic dates and will actually remember the anniversary of when you met.

But because he gets his feelings hurt easily (something you can reveal to your friends but never, ever to his!), throwing even the most constructive criticism his way will create a major riff in the relationship. At the core of any Pisces guy is the fear of being left broken-hearted. Once he starts to feel a relationship getting rocky, he will either bolt to spare himself the eventual heartache or almost suffocate you with attention to get things back on track. Show this easygoing guy how much you care, as often as you can, and you will have his heart.

pisces guy file

Where to spot him: Anywhere with a view

Win his heart by: Being careful of his easily bruised ego

Great date: Seeing an art exhibit

Major annoyance: Arguments

Astro matches: Cancer, Scorpio, Capricorn

Pisces hottie: Freddie Prinze Jr.

aries

(March 21 to April 19)

aries fast facts

Symbol: The Ram

Element: Fire

Ruling Planet: Mars

Color: Racy red

Flower: Thistle

Gemstone: Diamond

Day: Tuesday

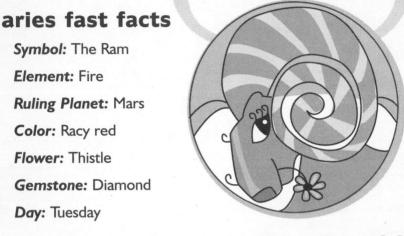

the aries girl

Ram girls are known for being high energy. You know, filling up your schedule with just about every activity imaginable, from sports to school clubs and whatever else you can squeeze into 24 hours. Unending stamina? You bet! Just about every other sign in the zodiac has trouble keeping up with the Ram.

Aries girls are also known for being, well, just a *little* on the competitive side. But so long as you're not a sore loser, there's nothing wrong with playing to win. You also tend to be pretty fearless—an attitude that lands you at the front of your pack of friends. It's not like you're trying to be the leader in every situation you encounter. It's just that your Ram-like qualities push you to the number one position.

aries stellar traits

Strengths: You can change a snore-fest into a rager with your winning personality.

Strikes: You can be fiercely competitive at times.

Loves: Anything adventurous and action-packed

Loathes: Losing

Looks: Casual clothes that can handle your active lifestyle

Hangout spot: The gym or the field

Soul mate: A guy who'll challenge you—mentally and physically

Friend trends: Those willing to follow your lead rank high in your social circle.

Movie match: *Buffy the Vampire Slayer*

Celebs who share your sign: Sarah Michelle Gellar, Melissa Joan Hart, Keri Russell, Reese Witherspoon, Julia Stiles, Robert Downey Jr., Jonathan Brandis

deep thoughts

With your leading lady status, you've got the world thinking you're cool and confident. And for the most part, you are. But even Aries girls get the blues. Difference is, you'd rather keep your probs under wraps than go whining to your girlfriends. You get over things by staying busy and getting completely immersed in doing things that distract you from your problems. All of which work quite well, thank you very much…up to a certain point. Just remember that most of your friends would do anything in the world for you (yup, Aries girls have that power), so when you wanna get things off your chest, give your pals a shout!

your social side

The worst thing about your social life? You're way overbooked. You get invited to nearly every party (who wouldn't want an Aries girl there to keep things from getting boring?), and you've somehow managed to get yourself signed up for every school committee there is. Plus you like to hang with your friends, try new activities, play sports—get the picture? And this is probably not news to you, but Aries girls rock when it comes to sports. Chalk it up to your confidence or your competitiveness—you're a fierce rival on the field.

On the friend front, you are by far one of the most honest and open signs. Because you are so willing to tell it like it is, your friends rely on you to give them a dose of reality when they most need it. Buds who can take your direct approach, like Geminis, Sagittarians, and Scorpios, are the easiest for you to get along with. Pal around with a more sensitive type and you're likely to hurt a few feelings now and then (which makes a friendship with a Pisces or Cancer girl tricky but certainly not impossible to navigate). On the plus side, your highly charged personality can draw even the shyest of signs out of their shells.

Friendly signs for Aries: Gemini, Scorpio, Sagittarius, Aquarius

star style

Like every other area of your life, you're willing to take the lead when it comes to finding fashions. And with your fab figure, just about any look will do you right. But no slave to style are you— if a look doesn't cut it in your mind, it won't make it into your closet.

matters of the heart

The good news, Aries: You'll probably never long for a date. In fact, at this very moment, there is probably more than one guy who is crushing on you…hard. The bad news: You'll have a hard time settling on that one special guy. And even when you do, your eyes might have the tendency to roam every now and then. As competitive as you are in all the other areas of your life, it's not surprising that you want a guy who's absolutely perfect. Reality check—he doesn't exist. (And if he *did*, you'd probably be bored with him in minutes, anyway.) But what *do* exist are plenty of great guys who can handle your need for excitement and passion in all areas of life…like a fun-loving Leo or a try-anything Sagittarius. You'll also meet your love match with an independent air sign—Gemini, Libra, or Aquarius. They'll give you just enough of a challenge, and you're the type of girl to get them to lighten up once in a while. While it may seem as though sensitive guys are not your style, you'd be surprised at how they can get you to open up and reveal the true you. So don't write off that Cancer or Pisces boy just yet!

the aries guy

Have your eyes on a Ram boy? Get ready for a wild ride. An Aries guy loves to be where the action is. Parties, playing sports, watching sports, school events—he'll make sure there's never a dull moment. He may seem a little hard to handle at times, but when you can get him to slow down and open up, you'll find that he has a totally romantic side as well. If you're the type who gets freaked out when your guy talks to other girls, this flirt-of-the-zodiac guy may not be your type. But just remember that when he's head over heels, he'll spoil you like no other sign.

If, on the other hand, an Aries guy has a crush on you, look out! Not one to give up easily, this guy will use his charm and personality endlessly in his pursuit of you.

aries guy file

Where to spot him: At sports practice

Win his heart by: Letting him know he's your one and only

Great date: Challenging him to a game of bowling

Major annoyance: Girls who obsess over their looks

Astro matches: Aquarius, Gemini, Sagittarius

Aries hottie: Hayden Christiansen

taurus

(April 20 to May 20)

taurus fast facts

Symbol: The Bull

Element: Earth

Ruling Planet: Venus

Color: Groovy green

Flower: Freesia

Gemstone: Topaz

Day: Friday

the taurus girl

Like the bull your sign is associated with, Taurus types are a wee bit stubborn. But why *would* you budge on your viewpoints? Being one of the most practical and sensible signs in the zodiac, you've probably got it all right anyway! You take time to analyze every situation, and you can read into a person's body-language signals to get to their true meaning.

The queen of justifying things, you're able to rationalize why you just have to have that electronic organizer. And boy, do Taurus girls like to have stuff! You have an eye for quality and can spot a knockoff Kate Spade bag from a mile away. Your exquisite taste extends to the guy front, too: Your crush choices are always hotties.

taurus stellar traits

Strengths: Your intense loyalty

Strikes: Your stubborn streak

Loves: Spending dough on your duds

Loathes: Anyone who's wishy-washy

Looks: Practical clothes in earthy hues to match your no-nonsense personality

Hangout spot: Poolside

Soul mate: A guy with strong opinions and an iron will

Friend trends: Be careful not to let little irritations snowball into major conflicts.

Movie match: *Girlfight*

Celebs who share your sign: Kirsten Dunst, Lance Bass, Danielle Fishel, Jason Biggs, David Boreanz

deep thoughts

There's a lot going on in the mind of a Taurus. Your brain is always set on play, absorbing convos, forming opinions, and coming up with clever assessments of situations. You like to get your way, if only because you really, really feel like your way is the best way. And until someone—and this goes for your parents as well as your friends—can convince you otherwise, you won't budge a bit on your viewpoint. Not surprisingly, this can cause a bit of conflict in your otherwise orderly world. You can also lose patience with friends whose problems seem so insignificant and ridiculous to you. Just remember that not everyone is blessed with Taurus sensibleness—so give your buds your common-sense advice and lend a much-needed shoulder to them.

your social side

Taurus girls are team players who also love to show off their own strengths for the crowd. You excel in sports and activities that involve others but that also let you shine individually. A team sport like softball or soccer gives you the combo you crave. Your idea of fun is a get-together with a few great friends that involves food, music, and girl gab. A crazed night on the town is not your idea of a good time. What's the point, you wonder, when you'd all have much more fun just hanging out?

You've got your social life organized pretty well and manage to get schoolwork done right on time so you can spend the evening chatting on the phone. Nothing rocks your world more, though, than an unexpected change to your schedule. And friends who bail on you at the list minute will, understandably, feel the wrath of the Bull's temper. No surprise you've got a bunch of stable friends, like you—friends who respect your feelings earn your closest confidence. A pal who's easygoing, like a Pisces or a Capricorn, can handle your methodical ways the best. Hanging around with an impulsive, unpredictable friend could cause a major freak-out on your part.

Friendly signs for Taurus: Cancer, Virgo, Libra, Capricorn, Pisces

star style

Taurus girls are the shopaholics of the zodiac. But you also approach the sport of shopping logically and methodically. While your friends are dropping bucks on bags full of random styles, you're sizing up stores for the best bargains on the quality stuff—items that will fit your existing wardrobe just perfectly. You have taste galore and appreciate what's well made and will last all season long. But just because you like good stuff doesn't mean your closet is filled with formal wear and high-style selections. *Au contraire*—Taurus girls practically invented casual wear. There's hardly a place for uncomfortable clothes in a Taurus girl's wardrobe.

taurus style sheet

Your best beauty feature: Your shiny, swinging mane

Look you'll love: A luxurious cashmere sweater set

Wouldn't be caught dead in: Anything trendy or faddish—you prefer timeless classics

Makeup item you can't live without: Black mascara

Scent pick: Floral fragrances with herbal undertones

Fashion diva: Gwyneth Paltrow

matters of the heart

There's nothing better to a Taurus girl than having a guy to call her own. Someone who'll snuggle with you nonstop and shower you with his affection is your definite astro-match. And while you do appreciate good looks and A-list qualities, most important to you is a guy's inner qualities. Your one weakness when it comes to love is jealousy—you want a guy who is so committed to you that he practically forgets there are other girls on the planet!

A Cancer or Pisces guy who can't seem to get enough of you will never grate on your nerves, while Virgo guys who share your same tastes will ensure that you get to do things you like to do. Guys you can connect with first as friends, like a

Capricorn or another Taurus, make for long-lasting love relationships. But the initial flame from a matchup with an Aries or a Sagittarius will die out as soon as their more adventurous side takes over. There may not be enough of a more-than-skin-deep connection when you connect with a Scorpio or an Aquarius—you want someone who can listen to your problems and tell you his.

the taurus guy

Headed into a relationship with a boy Bull? Here's what you need to know: Your typical Taurus guy can have a stubborn streak that can lead to constant commotion if you, too, like to be right. While he may be the last to give in, what he gives out can more than make up for it—the Taurus guy is devoted, romantic, and loyal. He's not much of a flirt, so if you're looking for a telltale sign that he likes you, better learn to read between the lines. He's also the type to keep his emotions well concealed. He really believes that you may bolt if you figure out how strong his feelings are for you. Since security is so important to him (yes, this guy really *likes* being in a relationship), he will end things if you tend to keep your guy options open by flirting nonstop.

taurus guy file

Where to spot him: The great outdoors

Win his heart by: Baking him cookies

Great date: Surprising him with a picnic

Major annoyance: Girls who flirt with anyone else

Astro matches: Virgo, Cancer, Pisces

Taurus hottie: Jeff Timmons of 98 Degrees

gemini

(May 21 to June 20)

gemini fast facts

Symbol: The Twins

Element: Air

Ruling Planet: Mercury

Color: Yummy yellow

Flower: Daisy

Gemstone: Tourmaline

Day: Wednesday

the gemini girl

Gemini girls are smart, sociable, and surrounded by good friends. Ruled by the Twins, Gemini girls are masters at handling more than one thing at a time—you can juggle homework while talking on the phone *and* watching *Friends*. A Gemini has got to be in constant motion lest she gets bored out of her mind—you've got energy to burn, baby. You have a wide variety of hobbies and interests and are always willing to give a new activity a try. Someone as clever as a Gemini never has too much trouble understanding schoolwork, although getting a good read on people's emotions is one area you could use a little help in. Fortunately, you don't have to do too much sleuthing to get the scoop on a situation since your friends are so ready to reveal just about anything to you. And if any sign rules the art of communication, it's you, Twin, as your cell phone bills will clearly attest!

gemini stellar traits

Strengths: You're an expert conversationalist and can persuade even a skeptical crowd to see things your way.

Strikes: You don't plan ahead.

Loves: Gadgets and gizmos

Loathes: Being bored

Looks: "The hipper, the better" is your style motto.

Hangout spot: A cyber café

Soul mate: A guy who knows when to smother you with kisses—and when to back off

Friend trends: They gotta be able to listen 'cause, girl, do you know how to talk!

Movie match: *The Matrix*

Celebs who share your sign: Courteney Cox Arquette, Joshua Jackson, Natalie Portman, Leelee Sobieski

deep thoughts

Geminis are quick-witted and clever, and your inquiring mind is always on the move to get more info. No wonder a Gemini is always talking. You like people—the more diverse, the better—and can work a party like a pro. But sitting still is no easy task for a restless Gemini, which is why you might have earned a reputation for being on the flighty side. People can mistake your need to mingle and then move on as a sign that you don't care. On the contrary—you're just trying to absorb as much as you can. Your curious nature can also lead to that—an inability to follow through on things. A girl can only do so much, though, right?

your social side

The Twin can take on a schedule that no other sign would be able to handle. You have a seemingly endless amount of energy. You're also clever as can be—a star student who has the ability to listen and to ask intelligent questions.

Since your energy supply is endless, you simply *must* make athletic activities a part of your life—the more rigorous, the better. While you might get bored senseless sitting in right field waiting for the ball to come your way, you can move your feet faster than anyone on the basketball court.

Friends are essential in a Gemini's world. You need to be constantly connected to your mates, and thanks to technology, you can stay in touch via cell phone, pager, and e-mail. The more interesting your pals, the better, which is why you and an Aries or Sagittarius girl get along so well. You find it easy to talk to an Aquarius or Scorpio and will have a nonstop good time with an equally social Libra. You've got a great sense of humor, and you expect your friends to have one, too, so an ultra-sensitive Cancer or Pisces pal might keep you on the defensive way too much.

Friendly signs for Gemini: Aries, Taurus, Libra, Scorpio, Aquarius

star style

A Gemini girl is fashion-forward and on the cutting edge. You are so into having the trendiest clothes that you'd practically sell your little sister—or at least her prized Hanson CD collection—to get your hands on the hottest new look. You're an MTV *House of Style* junkie and can actually name more than three famous designers (even if you can't afford them). You're like a salesperson's best friend, and when you walk into a store, in-the-know clerks clamor to help you. Like everything else in your life, you need variety in your wardrobe. You may turn up in jeans one day and a strappy little dress the next. But, hey—it's a girl's prerogative (and so essential for a Gemini!).

---

gemini style sheet

Your best beauty feature: Your pouty lips

Look you'll love: A pair of faux skin pants—you're way into funk

Wouldn't be caught dead in: Yesterday's fashion—you stay on top of the trends

Makeup item you can't live without: Shimmery silver high-lighting gel

Scent pick: Clean, fresh fragrances with undertones of flowers or citrus

Fashion diva: Kirsten Dunst

---

matters of the heart

Flirty Geminis may seem like they only want to have a good time, but they're just testing the water in search of a soul mate. All different kinds of guys seem interesting to you, so you rarely stick to just one clique when it comes to the dating pool. Guys might feel a little awkward asking you out, if only because they're intimidated by your confidence. It takes a gutsy guy to get up the nerve to ask a Gemini out, so if you've got your eye on someone shy, better make the first move yourself.

There's nothing worse to a Gemini than jealousy (which is kinda ironic, since your flirty personality lends itself to some suspicion), so a possessive Taurus or Pisces guy will be hard to take. Ditto that sensitive Cancer guy who gets bent out of shape when you look at other boys. You'll make an immediate connection with a fire sign—like a Leo, Aries, or Sagittarius—and another air sign, like a Libra or an Aquarius, will make cosmic chemistry.

the gemini guy

Having a hard time getting a read on whether that Gemini guy likes you or not? Here's the deal: Geminis may seem to have it totally together socially—anyone who's *that* talkative has got to be super-confident, right? But the truth is that while he *is* one of the most sociable signs, he doesn't necessarily have a grip on all of his emotions. In fact, he can be a little confused and overwhelmed by them, so that even when he *is* into you, he comes across as cool and distant. Your task, should you choose to take on this guy, is to learn to read between the lines, to get a sense for how he feels through things like body language and being around you more often. He longs to be understood and will find it easy to fall for a girl who has the ability to read his mind.

gemini guy file

Where to spot him: At a coffeehouse with his laptop

Win his heart by: Reading his mind

Great date: Dancing the night away

Major annoyance: Girls who don't listen

Astro matches: Leo, Libra, Aquarius

Gemini hottie: Joshua Jackson

cancer

cancer fast facts

Symbol: The Crab

Element: Water

Ruling Planet: The moon

Color: Sentimental silver

Flower: Peony

Gemstone: Moonstone

Day: Monday

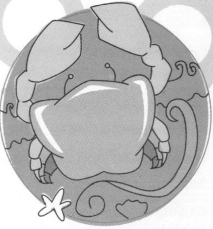

the cancer girl

Cancer girls got stuck with what seems to be the worst sign in the zodiac—not only does it share a name with a deadly disease, but the sign's symbol, a crab, is hardly the most desirable animal on the planet. Stinks to be you, right? Wrong! Cancer girls are actually way cool, from the way you can get friends to open up and spill all (can you say Oprah?) to the totally alluring spell you can cast on guys. You genuinely care about the people in your life. You can practically sense when someone is upset and will do everything you can to fix things for them (even if their problem has nothing to do with you, which is usually the case).

cancer stellar traits

Strengths: You're in touch with your intuition and use it wisely.

Strikes: You can't make up your mind.

Loves: Surfin' the Net

Loathes: Being put on the spot

Looks: You love the basics jazzed up with some vintage chic.

Hangout spot: Your bedroom

Soul mate: A guy who's shy but makes it obvious he adores you

Friend trends: You're the "Dear Abby" of your social circle.

Movie match: Never Been Kissed

Celebs who share your sign: Carson Daly, Josh Hartnett, Chris O'Donnell, Jessica Simpson, Prince William

deep thoughts

Cancer girls are ruled by the moon. As such, your moods can go from one extreme to another without warning. When you're up, you can be extremely sociable, chatting it up with friends and being the star of the social scene. But then there are those times when you need some serious "me time"—the times when you want to just hole up in your room, unplug your phone, and lose yourself in a book. Do yourself—and those around you—a favor and retreat when you feel the need. You'll come out of your homebound solitude with energy to spare.

At the core of a Cancer is a need to feel secure. Meeting new people or going to new places can rock your emotional boat. But once you get familiar with a face or a place, you let your inner charm come out.

your social side

Corny but true: A water sign like Cancer finds her true talent in activities associated with the wet stuff. If you haven't signed up for swim team yet, get on it! Though you may not be an all-around jock, playing sports is a good way for a Cancer girl to stay in the scene. Without structured activities and responsibilities, Cancers have the tendency to get a little lazy with their social lives. On the school and work front, though, the Cancer girl is anything but lazy. Not only are you smart and determined, you also hate to let anyone down, especially your family and teachers.

A Cancer can be an amazing, giving friend. You're a great listener who would drop everything to help a friend in need. The only thing about a Cancer that can cause waves in a friendship is your emotions. You can be soooooo sensitive, and your feelings get hurt easily. An air sign acquaintance—like a Gemini, Libra, or Aquarius—may be a little flighty for a Cancer girl, and you may have a tough time making a deeper connection. You prefer the company of a well-grounded earth sign, like a Taurus, Virgo, or Capricorn. Things will flow smoothly with a Pisces pal, and while an Aries friend may have more off-the-wall ideas than you're comfortable with, she'll be able to break you out of your shell every now and then to have a great time.

Friendly signs for Cancer: Aries, Taurus, Cancer, Virgo, Capricorn, Pisces

star style

A Cancer girl tends to mix emotions with clothes. You put a sentimental value on your styles—like the big comfy sweater that you snagged from your boyfriend's closet that makes you think of him every time you put it on. You can wear vintage looks like no other sign and like to shop boutiques and thrift stores to load up on oldies. What won't you see a Cancer girl wearing anytime soon? Flashy clothes that draw too much attention. Since you sometimes have trouble deciding what to wear, a closet that's got clothes that work well together—like basics or solid, mixable colors—will cure you of your clothes confusion.

cancer style sheet

Your best beauty feature: Your high and prominent cheekbones

Look you'll love: A beaded vintage bag—you love to complete your outfit with a signature accessory

Wouldn't be caught dead in: Loud colors or patterns—you like your fashion soft and subtle

Makeup item you can't live without: Long-lasting cream blush

Scent pick: Classic, romantic scents that are long-lasting and big on flowers

Fashion diva: Jessica Simpson

matters of the heart

Cancers are definitely not commitment shy. One of the most romantic signs in the zodiac, you have a strong desire to shower someone with love and affection. Not only do you need to show your affection, you also need to be on the receiving end of someone's romantic ways. That said, you need a guy who likes to both give and get when it comes to relationships. To a Cancer, the end of a relationship can be the end of the world. In fact, you're so in love with the idea of being in love that you might just settle for someone who's beneath your standards.

Instead of getting stuck with a date who's a dud, try pairing up with an astrological soul mate, like the gentle and loving Pisces or the sweet and smart Capricorn. You might have some intense times with a Scorpio sweetie, but you—yes you, Cancer girl, believe it or not—can start to feel a little stifled. You'll want to douse those fire-sign flames—Aries, Leo, and Sagittarius—with a little water to tone them down a notch, but they may find you too tame to make this a strong match. A Gemini guy may not be willing to commit to you, but with a Virgo or a Taurus, you'll find a guy who's not only cool with commitment but way into your ways.

the cancer guy

Want to connect with a sensitive Crab guy? Show him how much you adore him, and don't be shy about it! A Cancer guy can't stand rejection and will try to conceal his true emotions until he's certain of where he stands with you. When he's ready to take the plunge and make a commitment, though, you'll be one of the luckiest girls alive. This guy knows how to play the romantic lead in a relationship. He won't be afraid to plant one on your lips, even in front of his guy friends. The one drawback is his tendency to be moody. He can get into funks for no apparent reason, and no matter what you try, you won't be able to get him back to focusing his full attention on you. Just give him time, though, and he'll work things out on his own. If you can get past his mood swings, you're in for some serious pampering.

cancer guy file

Where to spot him: At the pool

Win his heart by: Getting along with his mom

Great date: Renting a kayak

Major annoyance: Being teased

Astro matches: Taurus, Scorpio, Pisces

Cancer hottie: Tobey Maguire

leo

leo fast facts

Symbol: The Lion

Element: Fire

Ruling Planet: The sun

Color: Glam gold

Flower: Red rose

Gemstone: Cat's-eye

Day: Sunday

the leo girl

Leo is ruled by the sun—the center of the universe, which could explain why a Leo girl feels the need to be the center of attention! The original drama queen, a Leo knows how to draw attention her way, be it by flashing that too-charming smile of hers or doling out the school's juiciest gossip. Somewhat of a show-off, a Leo prides herself on her accomplishments and social skills. But don't think you're coming off conceited, Lion girl—here's the real deal: Everyone really *is* dazzled by your amazing personality. Your friends rely on you to liven up even the dullest of get-togethers, and guys find your playfulness refreshing. Besides, though it's mostly about "me, me, me," you would never be disloyal to any of your friends, and they know it.

leo stellar traits

Strengths: You know how to take charge and always have fab ideas.

Strikes: You think you're the center of the universe.

Loves: Being in the limelight

Loathes: Anything ordinary

Looks: If it glows, glitters, sparkles, or shines, you'll be wearing it.

Hangout spot: The video store

Soul mate: A guy who'll put you first—and not outshine you

Friend trends: You're a loyal gal pal, but you're snarly when crossed.

Movie match: *Center Stage*

Celebs who share your sign: Ben Affleck, J.C. Chasez, Lisa Kudrow, Drew Lachey, Matt LeBlanc, Matthew Perry

deep thoughts

Is there a hidden meaning behind all this self-motivation? Let's just say the Leo girl needs to be adored by others. Your self-confidence (and you *do* have it) stems from the reaction you get from those around you. Because you're so intent on being in front of the spotlight, looking good is a priority. You have a drawer full of Cliniqué, Lancome, and Laura Mercier makeup (only the best for you, Lion girl), and rarely is a hair out of place in your up-to-date 'do. You're also not afraid to tell it like it is, even when your opinions can get you into trouble. But you're well aware of the fact that being blunt gives you a social edge and makes your friends admire you even more.

your social side

It's not unusual for a Leo to be all over the school's yearbook. You're definitely not camera-shy. But even more than that, a Leo girl appears everywhere in the annual because she's involved in just about everything. A natural leader, you're found chairing committees, presiding over clubs, and heading up the squad. Speaking of squads, there's no better candidate for school cheerleader than a Leo. And while some girls are reluctant to raise their hands in class, a Leo will throw out an answer whether she's sure of it or not. Such enthusiasm makes her a teacher's pet and ensures the Leo of good grades.

Leos need the undying support and attention of their friends, and those who are put off by your pushy behavior are probably better off as acquaintances. Beyond your attention-getting ways, though, is a friend who is extremely devoted and loyal. You click cosmically with signs that understand and appreciate you, like any easygoing Libra or an on-the-move Sagittarius. You're at first intrigued by a Capricorn's need to keep you focused on your goals and an Aquarian's way of life constantly keeping you in line, but the phase will quickly pass and annoyance will set in. A Pisces may seem too dull for you at first, but you'll quickly see that she's a friend who brings out the best in you—and that's what's best for you.

Friendly signs for Leo: Libra, Sagittarius, Pisces

star style

What better way to stand out than with the most amazing wardrobe? To a Leo, clothes are yet another means to be the center of attention, so you look for styles that turn heads. You're not afraid of a little sparkle and shine in your wardrobe, so things like shiny animal-skin prints, glittered accessories, and bold, metallic colors are standard items on your shopping list. You aren't exactly the best at shopping bargain basement stores, preferring to shop places that will give you personal attention. You like to bring friends along on your shopping sprees, if only to ooh and ahh at you when you emerge from the fitting room.

leo style sheet

Your best beauty feature: Your sparkling eyes

Look you'll love: A pair of spike-heeled sandals that show off your perfect pedicure

Wouldn't be caught dead in: Clothes that make you blend into the crowd—you like to stand out

Makeup item you can't live without: Smudgy kohl eye pencil

Scent pick: Musk or strong floral undertones that have staying power

Fashion diva: Britney Spears

matters of the heart

Leos put their hearts on the line easily and tend to fall in love frequently. The whole idea of courtship—getting flowers, long phone calls, and sweet cards—seems as though it were created for a Leo. You just love to be showered with all that attention. But someone who is so quick to give away her heart is also vulnerable to heartbreak, so beware of boys who seem to enjoy the pursuit of capturing a Lion more than they long for the kind of commitment you crave.

Your ultimate love match is a Capricorn, who'll make you feel amazingly special without over-bloating your ego. A Libra or a Gemini can also charm you, and the initial flirt-fest will have your head spinning. A Virgo or a Taurus might be too down-to-earth for your taste, while one of the water signs—Cancer, Scorpio, or Pisces—may give you just the right dose of passion (so long as they don't get over-sensitive and jealous). The heat will really be on if you make a love connection with another Leo or a fire sign, like an Aries or Sagittarius. Just get ready for a wild and nonstop ride.

the leo guy

Think you can tame a Lion? Better know how to appreciate him the way he needs to be appreciated...meaning all the time! A Leo guy can be a bit of a show-off, and he'll be watching to see if you notice him. (Who can resist that charm and personality?!) The type of girl who Leos are attracted to is one who's confident and a little hard-to-get. The king of the jungle has to feel as though he's hooked himself a real prize. But like the animal that rules his sign, this Lion can also be fiercely loyal. When he's in love, he'll work hard to impress you and will show you how much he cares with cards and notes—one shoe box will not be enough to hold everything this guy will give you! While you may be dying for a quiet night together, he'll want to take you out on the town and show you off to his friends—so don't expect too many solo dates with this social guy.

leo guy file

Where to spot him: On stage

Win his heart by: Giving him tons of compliments

Great date: A double feature

Major annoyance: Not being noticed

Astro matches: Aries, Libra, Gemini

Leo hottie: Ben Affleck

virgo

(August 23 to September 22)

virgo fast facts

Symbol: The Virgin

Element: Earth

Ruling Planet: Mercury

Color: Bold blue

Flower: Tulip

Gemstone: Peridot

Day: Wednesday

the virgo girl

It's all about order for the particular, perfectionist Virgo, and you've got a list of pet peeves to prove it: Sloppiness, laziness, and being late annoy you to no end. But will you write off friends who can't seem to get their acts together? Oh, no. Yours is the sign of service, so instead you'll try to help those unorganized souls get it together!

The Virgo girl can be a neat freak. One quick look at your locker or at the way you have your photos organized by category should be a clear indication that your birthday falls under the sign of the Virgin. Your neatness extends to your looks as well—your makeup is probably stashed in an organizer and your clothes arranged in closet by color. You take pride in maintaining a healthy lifestyle, and you fit regular workouts into your meticulously organized planner.

virgo stellar traits

Strengths: You know how to view probs objectively.

Strikes: You're picky, picky, picky.

Loves: Getting—and staying—organized

Loathes: Sloppiness

Looks: Perfectly polished

Hangout spot: The library

Soul mate: A guy who's smart and easygoing

Friend trends: You give great advice, but be careful not to be a doormat.

Movie match: *You've Got Mail*

Celebs who share your sign: Cameron Diaz, Brad Fischetti, Ryan Phillipe, Carly Pope, Jada Pinkett Smith, Scott Speedman

deep thoughts

At the core of a Virgo's over-the-top organization is a need to be in control. It's important to you that things are in order, lest you start to feel overwhelmed. Life being what it is, though, you are likely to be thrown a curveball every now and then. That's when the anxiety kicks in, and that shell starts to crack. A dose of meditation or yoga can help you stay cool—why not pencil in some Eastern therapy into your schedule? You sometimes set impossibly high standards for yourself, and when you inevitably can't live up to them, you feel like you've let the world down. Sometimes, Virgo girl, you just need to lighten up and appreciate the amazing qualities you possess.

your social side

Virgos are way into self-improvement, so the hobbies and activities you tend to sign up for are those that can make you a better person. You no doubt have a membership or access to a gym, or take part in a sport like running or swimming to stay in shape. Because you're so helpful, you make a great team-mate—one who does things for the good of the team and not her own gain.

Good grades are also important to you, and you cringe when you mess up on a test or paper. But since academics are key to a Virgo, you come to class well-prepared. You'd never forego doing your homework if something more fun came along.

Your friends can always rely on you to set them straight when they start to stray down the wrong path. You give them a dose of reality when they most need it. You can also get a shy girl like a Cancer to come out of her shell and open up to you. Ditto the sometimes stubborn Taurus—once you get her talking, the two of you will never be able to get off the phone! You want only the best for your buds, but to a friend who's another Virgo or an Aquarius, your advice might come off as insulting. With a fun-loving Leo or an adventure-minded Aries, you'll be put in charge of planning what is sure to be a night you won't forget.

Friendly signs for Virgos: Taurus, Cancer, Libra, Aquarius, Pisces

star style

A Virgo girl can make a pair of vintage Levi's look spectacular. You know just how to put an outfit together and wouldn't dream of walking out the door without having every hair in place. Your stable of accessories includes classics and up-to-date extras that dress up any outfit. Your clothes have a timeless appeal to them; turtlenecks and jeans have taken you through times when you just couldn't stand the other available trends. You look great in solid colors like navy, green, white, and the backbone of your wardrobe—basic black. You're a picky shopper, so your friends better have patience when they hit the mall with you!

virgo style sheet

Your best beauty feature: Your swanlike neck

Look you'll love: A pair of knee-high black leather boots that will take you anywhere

Wouldn't be caught dead in: Clothes that are baggy or sloppy —for you, neatness counts

Makeup item you can't live without: Classic red lipstick

Scent pick: Fragrances with floral, fruit, citrus, or vanilla notes

Fashion diva: Lucy Liu

matters of the heart

The picky Virgo is quite particular about the guys she dates. You'd rather stay home and watch *Rugrats* with your baby brother than go on a duty date with a guy you couldn't care less about. But just like anyone with a pulse, when you do fall for someone, all logic seems lost as your emotions take over, especially when you start to mistakenly believe that you aren't good enough for him. (When, in fact, it's usually the opposite!) Because your shy streak comes out when you encounter a new situation, you may come across to guys as being uninterested. But keep in mind that this may make them try even harder to win your heart.

You'll find relationship bliss with a guy whose standards are as high as yours, like a Taurus, a Capricorn, or another Virgo, while a fiery Scorpio, Aries, or Aquarius will get high-voltage sparks shooting. (Can you handle all that excitement? It'll be fun finding out, at least.) The sweet words a Pisces or Cancer guy will say to you will make you float on air, but when you're back on solid ground, you may find them a little too dreamy. Since you're such a loyal and trusting person, you may be put off by how much a Leo or a Libra will test your tolerance.

the virgo guy

Virgo males are super-selective. Their ideal girl has got to have it all together—looks, personality, brains—the whole enchilada. This Mr. Fix-it can also spot a diamond in the rough, so beware the boy who seems to think he has to help you improve upon your already impressive qualities.

Virgo guys are the best dressed in the zodiac, if only because, unlike a lot of guys, they actually care about how they look. He might even ask you for your opinion on what to wear—yikes! He can sometimes seem a little too perfect—and could use a girl with some spunk to get him out of his neat-freak funk. Your mom will give this guy a major thumbs-up, which may make you worry a little. But before you write him off as being too nerdy for your taste, get him engaged in some serious conversation and get to know the real perceptive and, yes, even passionate, Virgo guy.

virgo guy file

Where to spot him: At the hardware store

Win his heart by: Being on time

Great date: Take him on a long bike ride

Major annoyance: Sloppiness

Astro matches: Capricorn, Taurus, Cancer

Virgo hottie: Ryan Phillipe

libra

(September 23 to October 22)

libra fast facts

Symbol: The Scales

Element: Air

Ruling Planet: Venus

Color: Passionate pink

Flower: Iris

Gemstone: Opal

Day: Friday

the libra girl

Someone whose sign is the Scales can't help but crave balance and harmony. You try to fix what's not working—from your friends' relationships to your boyfriend's inability to commit. Your sign is also a sociable one, and you love nothing more than hanging out with your friends or mingling with a crowd of soon-to-be sisters. You loathe being alone; thankfully, you rarely are.

Your ruling planet being Venus, planet of beauty and style, you also take pains to ensure you look good. You are on top of the trends—the best-dressed girl in school, no doubt.

libra stellar traits

Strengths: You're full of charm and charisma.

Strikes: You can be kinda clingy.

Loves: Getting picked for the team

Loathes: Conflict

Looks: Feminine, but not frilly

Hangout spot: The local art museum

Soul mate: A guy who'll tell you how great you look

Friend trends: You dig intense friendships, but everyone needs some space, including you.

Movie match: *Charlie's Angels*

Celebs who share your sign: Neve Campbell, Rachael Leigh Cook, Matt Damon, Gwyneth Paltrow, Kevin Richardson, Alicia Silverstone, Will Smith, Kate Winslet

deep thoughts

There's a lot more for a Libra girl to be proud of than just her awesome fashion sense. While you love being complimented for looking good, you know that it's what's on the inside that matters more. Every once in a while, you wish someone would take a look past those designer labels to see the real you. You're a people-pleaser by nature—you try to find the good in others and let them know it. Some people wonder if your intentions are true. When they get to know the real you, they'll see you're 100 percent genuine. The need for peace makes you try to rationalize everything, including other people's not-so-nice behavior. It's OK, Libra girl, to let your inner Buffy out when somebody does you wrong.

your social side

Libras feel best when they are surrounded by their buddies. No solo activities for this social star—you'd much rather get involved in sports, clubs, and organizations where you can interact with others. You've also got an artistic side that you rarely take the time to explore. Instead, you let your creativity come out via that impressive fashion sense.

You want your friendships to be conflict-free; girls who seem ready to stir things up all the time will soon find themselves out of your circle. (Your willingness to help make peace only goes so far.) A Sagittarius will provide tons of fun times, but her bluntness can offend if she doesn't know when to bite her tongue. You can relate to friends who will listen to you with an open mind and not be quick to pass judgment on you or anyone else. In other words, Libra girls just want to have a good time. You'll have tons of that with a Virgo or an Aquarius pal. Water signs, like Cancer, Scorpio, and Pisces, are the perfect listeners for the ever-so-talkative Libra, and they share your desire to see things in a positive light. (Though at times, a Cancer or Pisces pal can seem a little clingy.) If you're friends with a Leo, get ready for the world's longest phone conversations. She can talk as much as you! Still, though, you'll feel flattered when she seeks your opinion and advice on just about everything.

Friendly signs for Libras: Taurus, Leo, Cancer, Scorpio, Virgo, Aquarius

star style

The gentle and refined Libra has a clothes challenge—finding up-to-date styles that still show off your feminine side. You prefer soft fabrics (think knits, angora, suede) and flattering styles. (No baggy pants here, thank you very much.) On the other hand, you can pull off sweat pants and make them look alluring (rolling down the waist just so to reveal a bit of belly—get the picture?). Light colors in both clothes and makeup are ultra-flattering for you, Libra girl. But lest your look starts to get a little boring, rev up your kinda conservative clothes with some off-the-wall accessories, like a bold print purse or clunky, funky shoes.

libra style sheet

Your best beauty feature: Your well-manicured hands

Look you'll love: A flowing floral shawl—you look for clothes that are romantic

Wouldn't be caught dead in: Clothes that are mannish— you're pure femininity

Makeup item you can't live without: Tinted moisturizer

Scent pick: A fragrance that has floral or woodsy undertones

Fashion diva: Cameron Diaz

matters of the heart

Libras are great conversationalists, which makes meeting guys a cinch. You know the importance of being friends with a guy first, and you don't get all tongue-tied the second he lets you know he's interested. The girl who strives for harmony in her world really does crave being in a solid relationship—and nothing drives you crazier than being on the receiving end of some guy's head games. In a relationship, you can be one of the most romantic signs. You keep your sweetie walking on air with gushy cards and creative dates, like sending your guy on a treasure hunt to locate tickets for a hockey game.

With other air signs, like Gemini, Aquarius, or even another Libra, you'll find the right amount of mental stimulation and a similar desire to get together with friends for fun times. Ditto a match with a Sagittarius or a Leo. You can be just as unpredictable as an Aries guy, but a dose of his own medicine might drive him nuts. With a sensitive water boy (a Cancer, Scorpio, or Pisces), it'll be his ups and downs that start to grate. Might be better to find someone a little more grounded, like a Taurus or Virgo.

the libra guy

Oh, to get a Libra guy to commit! While his sign is one of the most romantic, this boy can be a little fickle, to say the least. But if he's into you, he'll pile on the praise and attention like no other. Because he's such a friendly guy, you may start to feel as though he's flirting with every one of your friends, and your lack of trust will drive him nuts—especially since he showers you with attention and romance every chance he gets. He digs a girl who's confident and has her own hobbies and interests aside from him. He still, though, totally wants you to show him how much you appreciate him and will gloat about his girl to his friends. And though the Libra guy can come off as confident, friendly, and flirty, he's secretly scared of being on his own.

libra guy file

Where to spot him: At an art museum

Win his heart by: Showing him he's appreciated

Great date: Join him for an intense game of racquetball

Major annoyance: Girls who are insensitive

Astro matches: Sagittarius, Aquarius, Gemini

Libra hottie: Backstreet Boy Kevin Richardson

scorpio

(October 23 to November 21)

scorpio fast facts

Symbol: The Scorpion

Element: Water

Ruling Planet: Pluto

Color: Outrageous red

Flower: Orchid

Gemstone: Ruby

Day: Tuesday

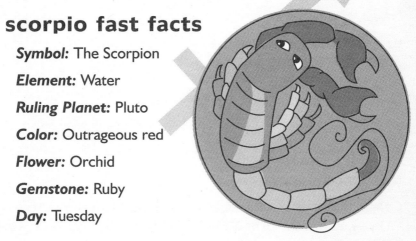

the scorpio girl

The Scorpio girl is mysterious and deep—the kind of girl you can know for years but never really know. This secretive side can keep the guys guessing, too. It seems like everyone wants to get inside the Scorpio mind. Take a number, folks—Scorpio won't be revealing secrets anytime soon.

You have a compassionate, caring side that makes you a great friend and the kind of girlfriend guys never get over. (Your high school beau will probably try and track you down long after you've graduated from college...just to see if there might still be a chance for something.) Your determination also helps you take control of situations and conquer any challenge you take on. Forget the train that *thought* it could; you *know* you can.

scorpio stellar traits

Strengths: You're caring and compassionate.

Strikes: You have an evil temper.

Loves: Winning an argument

Loathes: Being interrupted

Looks: Classic, but with a twist

Hangout spot: That ragin' new boutique

Soul mate: A guy who's not intimidated by your intense personality

Friend trends: You can be so possessive.

Movie match: *Scary Movie*

Celebs who share your sign: Leslie Bibb, Leonardo DiCaprio, Daisy Fuentes, Ethan Hawke, Nick Lachey, Tara Reid, Julia Roberts

deep thoughts

Someone so private as you, Scorp, has got to have a lot going on in her mind. And yes, oh yes, can that brain of yours enter its own world! Creative endeavors like painting or writing can help you hone in on that imaginative energy of yours and pull you out of those slumps when you turn into a loner. And by all means, keep a journal! Like other water signs, you are highly intuitive. Even though you're a hard read, everyone else is practically transparent to you. That's the reason fake friends could never be considered close to a Scorpio. One of the more emotional signs, you've learned how to make your feelings work for you. You get what you want by becoming who you need to be. Yup, Scorpio, you can be hard to take at times but are well worth putting up with!

your social side

A Scorpio is always on the go, doing something productive. Fortunately, you've determined that shopping is a useful endeavor. A girl's gotta have clothes, right? But you don't just hit one store and call it a day. Oh, no—the Scorpio girl can turn the task into a daylong shop-a-thon. Scorpios also prefer hands-on activities, not passive pastimes, and you do well in classes that let you explore things on your own. You'd much rather do a research project on the Civil War than answer a multiple-choice test on the subject. Fitness is important to you, too, and you despise laziness in yourself and others.

While you are an incredibly supportive and reliable friend (the flakiness factor of a Scorpio is practically nonexistent), you do not, repeat NOT, put up with friends who break that ever-so-important Scorpion trust. (Wanna feel the Scorpio's sting? Just try blabbing her secrets.) A friendship with a Cancer or Pisces, who can read your mind but would never reveal your thoughts, will be rock-solid. Because you never like to sit still, friends with a strong sense of adventure will make life even more interesting for you, which is why Scorpios often bond best with Aries or Sagittarius buds. But pure only takes the Scorpion so far—you want to be able to have deep and meaningful conversations at the same time. Will a Leo girl relate? Maybe not. Your idealism will make a friendship with an Aquarius or another Scorpio one that reaps huge altruistic rewards.

Friendly signs for Scorpio: Aries, Cancer, Libra, Sagittarius, Aquarius, Pisces

star style

Fuzzy, fluffy sweaters absolutely line a Scorpio girl's closet. That's 'cause not only is comfort a priority, but you also know that you've got it and don't need to flaunt it. No matter what you put on, your passionate, feminine side shows through—which is why you're able to shop the guys' departments and load up on sweaters and other basics that would cost a lot more in the girls' department. Your fave wardrobe item is probably a boy sweater. But while you're able to find tomboy styles to flatter, you still like to feel sexy—and you'll hit trendy stores as soon as that Structure purchase is rung up.

scorpio style sheet

Your best beauty feature: Your intense eyes

Look you'll love: A versatile wool sweater you can throw over everything

Wouldn't be caught dead in: Anything frilly—your femininity shows through without fuss

Makeup item you can't live without: Concealer

Scent pick: A warm and spicy fragrance, like vanilla

Fashion diva: Reese Witherspoon

matters of the heart

Scorpios are not short on intense feelings...once they let themselves fall for a guy, that is. You can be methodical about who you'll decide is worthy of your affection. But once you find the one, you'll win him over with a dose of your Scorpion intensity. Your biggest relationship problem is that your possessive nature can make you almost smother a guy. Here's the deal: Most guys fall harder for you than you do for them. He'll be completely stricken, so don't get all stressed about whether he's committed or not. Chances are, he's so devoted it probably scares him. A relationship with a water sign, like yours, will start off strong, but beware his possessiveness—you can dish it out but hate to take it yourself. Get ready for some emotional drama with a fiery Aries or Sagittarius—you'll give him guilt trips and he'll give you headaches. Friendships with a Capricorn, Virgo, or Taurus type can lead to earth-shattering relationships (in a good way, that is). Because you really are practical at heart, the untamed ways of an Aquarius or Gemini guy can make you a little uneasy. A Libra guy, though, knows how to balance his wild side—it just might work with him!

the scorpio guy

Can you handle the most passionate and intense sign in the zodiac? A Scorpio is a one-girl type of guy who's at his best when he's got a girlfriend. Because he's a little insecure, he can get possessive with you. Do yourself a favor and squelch that clingy behavior before it makes you feel too tied down. That old insecurity also makes it tough for him to tell you his true feelings—he wants you to tell him how much you like him before he reveals that he can't live without you. A Scorpio guy may be able to forgive, but he never forgets. Cheat on him and the relationship is over.

One thing that drives a Scorpio guy crazy is a girl who gossips about her relationship to friends. (Hello?! Who doesn't do that?) He wants to believe that the bond you two share stays between the two of you. So let him think that…you don't have to tell your guy *everything*, do you?

scorpio guy file

Where to spot him: The latest hot spot

Win his heart by: Giving him lots of affection

Great date: Seeing a hot new band

Major annoyance: Being criticized

Astro matches: Pisces, Taurus, Capricorn

Scorpio hottie: BBMak's Mark Barry

sagittarius

(November 22 to December 21)

sagittarius fast facts

Symbol: The Centaur

Element: Fire

Ruling Planet: Jupiter

Color: Powerful purple

Flower: Daisy

Gemstone: Lapis lazuli

Day: Thursday

the sagittarius girl

Where's the party? Just follow a Sagittarius girl and you'll wind up somewhere fun. Sag girls are out to have a rockin' good time. If you had a personal motto, it would be "Don't fence me in, baby." It's all about freedom for the socially gifted Centaur. You know how to laugh at your own mistakes and can easily take constructive criticism—so you totally can't understand why people get bent out of shape when you, in turn, tell it like it is. Especially because you never say anything maliciously— you tend to see the good in people and what may be perceived by others as an insult is meant by you as more of a helpful hint. You are, though, an incredibly loyal pal. If anyone ever tried to talk down to you about one of your friends, you'd quickly come to her defense.

sagittarius stellar traits

Strengths: You're the life of the party.

Strikes: You're not always reliable.

Loves: Embarking on a new adventure

Loathes: Being tied down

Looks: Comfy, yet alluring

Hangout spot: The beach

Soul mate: A guy who can keep up with your high energy

Friend trends: You're partial to people who share your appetite for adventure.

Movie match: Vertical Limit

Celebs who share your sign: Christina Aguilera, Aaron Carter, Katie Holmes, Lucy Liu, Brad Pitt, Britney Spears

deep thoughts

Sagittarians always seem to be in good moods. Not much gets you down. You like being around people and get energized in group situations. While some girls need private time to gather their thoughts, you prefer putting things into place with the help of close friends. You're optimistic about life and about other people, and you're completely honest about your feelings. In fact, sometimes you don't realize when you've hurt a friend's feelings and can seem a little indifferent when a sensitive sort asks for an apology. (Here's a tip: Try saying, "Sorry," instead of, "Well, sooooorrry!")

your social side

If a Sagittarius girl had it her way, she'd spend all her time away from home—traveling, hanging with friends, and meeting new people. Your urge to wander means that you're always on the go—mentally, too, which can make sitting in class for endless lectures a task Sagittarians can barely endure. You excel at oral exams, and while you may not be the first to volunteer to be the leader of a school project, you'll gradually step up to the plate when someone needs you. Athletics and activities are a hugely important part of your busy social sked. You do well in team sports and are an awesome defensive player.

A Sagittarius girl can never seem to understand why so many of her girlfriends get in fights. To you, most of the stuff they spar over is totally trivial. You prefer your friendships to be hassle-free. Your tendency to tell it like it is, though, can sometimes put you in the center of the conflict—a friend who can take your honest assessments without getting freaked out will give you the friendship harmony you need. You'll have an easy time with an Aries, Taurus, or another Sagittarius. While a Libra can have a tough time taking your blunt remarks, the sometimes-sensitive Cancer will see that you mean no harm. (And she will defend you when other girls get bent out of shape about your behavior.) A Leo friendship connection can produce a little friendly rivalry and a lot of outrageous good times. Because you're good at getting people to lighten up, you'll make even the most serious of Geminis or Capricorns laugh nonstop.

Friendly signs for Sagittarius: Aries, Taurus, Cancer, Leo, Sagittarius

star style

Sag girls are masters at layering clothes, important for one of the most active signs in the zodiac. You'll wear a sweater over your outfit in class, tie it around your waist for after-school activities, then throw it over your shoulders for a date with your guy. Your clothes have got to be as easygoing as you are, which is why your wardrobe staple is jeans. (A girl can never have too many pairs, right?) You love accessories for brightening up all those basics you own, but when they start to feel constricting, they wind up in the bottom of your bag. Sags are also big spenders and can blow through money at the mall before your friends have even finished finding outfit #1.

sagittarius style sheet

Your best beauty feature: Your button nose

Look you'll love: A perfectly cut pair of jeans

Wouldn't be caught dead in: Anything tight or uncomfortable—you need looks that let you move freely

Makeup item you can't live without: Lip liner

Scent pick: Fresh, clean fragrances that aren't too heavy

Fashion diva: Katie Holmes

matters of the heart

A Sagittarius girl needs intellectual stimulation from a relationship. All brawn and no brains in a boy would bore you to tears. You like a challenge, too, and will go after the school's most eligible guy with a vengeance. Once he falls for you, though, you're likely to start looking for your next romantic challenge. You also prefer to be out having fun. Romantic, one-on-one dates are great for the first few weeks, but after that, you're ready to go out in a group. Opposites, though, sometimes *do* attract, and you could find that the solo Scorpio guy has a mystery about him you'd love to spend time figuring out. A guy who tries to push you to get serious too soon (which a Pisces or Cancer guy might) or control you (which can be so very Virgo-like) will be history before date number two. Since you have a tendency to look before you leap, a guy who's well-grounded can save you from getting into too much trouble. Enter the Aries guy—your not-too-stuffy savior—or the Taurus guy with his mellow nature. The good times will never end with a Leo or another Sag; and it's you, only you, who can use your charisma to get a hard-to-figure-out Aquarius to expose his true feelings.

the sagittarius guy

When you think Sagittarius guy, think Brad Pitt: honest, intense, adventurous, and independent. (Not a bad thing to have to think about!) As much as you want to make Brad Pitt yours, this guy is not for everyone. Realize that and you can save yourself some unnecessary heartache. If you do hook up with a Sagittarius guy, get ready to let loose. He's up for an adventure and wants the one he's with to join in on the fun as well.

The Sag guy needs his space, too, so don't be offended if he tells it to you like it is and asks for some solo time. (If your feelings are easily hurt, you're gonna have to develop a thick skin to stay with him. Sagittarius guys are honest and blunt.) When he's done retreating from the relationship, he'll more than make up for time missed. But even though he does require going on relationship breaks, he really loves being in coupledom and wants to find that special girl who can take him just the way he is.

sagittarius guy file

Where to spot him: An arcade

Win his heart by: Giving him his own space

Great date: Going to an amusement park

Major annoyance: Girls who pressure him to commit before he's ready

Astro matches: Libra, Aries, Aquarius

Sagittarius hottie: Brad Pitt

capricorn

(December 22 to January 19)

capricorn fast facts

Symbol: The Goat

Element: Earth

Ruling Planet: Saturn

Color: Funky green

Flower: Lilac

Gemstone: Onyx

Day: Saturday

the capricorn girl

Ambition and achievement are what drives the serious, hard-working Goat. Not only are you determined, but you are extremely disciplined. Even if your friends called with some amazing gossip, you'd wait until your homework was done before you phoned them back. You're also known to be on the conservative side—your parents don't need to worry too much about you throwing a party the second they leave town. You've got the same sensibilities when it comes to dating. If a guy wants to get to know you better, he'd better call you and set up a date.

Getting good grades (and hence that acceptance letter to an Ivy League school) is important to you, and you tend to judge yourself based on what you accomplish. You also think the rest of world is judging you by what you achieve. Little do you know, others value your drive, determination, and honesty above all else.

capricorn stellar traits

Strengths: You're determined and self-disciplined.

Strikes: You can be overly cautious and hypersensitive.

Loves: Acing tests

Loathes: Procrastination

Looks: Tried-and-true traditional

Hangout spot: Your bedroom

Soul mate: A guy who's honest, smart, and shares your work ethic.

Friend trends: Pals always come to you for advice, and you're happy to help.

Movie match: *Dead Poet's Society*

Celebs who share your sign: Jason Behr, Jim Carrey, Jude Law, Ricky Martin, Kate Moss, Tyrese, Tiger Woods

deep thoughts

Ever so hardworking, the Capricorn girl can forget to take a breather every now and then to have a good time. Your friends constantly prod you to put away the books and hit the mall, but you rarely budge. Just remember, Goat girl, to schedule fun into your life. Capricorns also have the tendency to be status-conscious. You have a hard time seeing the good in people who don't know how to package themselves well. Because you take time to analyze things (and you really, really get it right much of the time), you can get a bit miffed when your friends don't agree with you. You'll spend waaaay too much time trying to change their point of view to yours.

your social side

The productive, plodding Capricorn girl may not seem like your perfect candidate for a rockin' good time. And when your mind is on something else (like school, work, or whatever else needs to get done), you're in no mood for fun. When you *do* set aside time for pleasure (and, yup—you usually schedule in friends and fun), you make sure that everyone is having an excellent time. You prefer to be the one doing the planning, and you're darn good at it, too. A Capricorn's knack for planning extends to her extracurricular activities as well, and you'd be the perfect candidate for heading up your school's social committee (further proof that you make a business out of having fun). Of course, you'd make an even better student body prez, so consider aiming for higher office, if you so desire.

On the friend front, Capricorns are known to be the unspoken leaders of their social circles. Friends often defer to you for advice or to be the one to call everyone up and make plans. The one activity you have a tough time getting into is hanging out for the sake of hanging out—you'd much rather be doing something or going somewhere. A friend who shares that need for nonstop stimulation makes a great Goat girlfriend, and Aries, Leo, Sagittarius, or other Capricorn girls will deliver. You may be straitlaced (most of the time), but you have the ability to understand the eccentricities of others, like an Aquarius or a Scorpio. Your astro opposite, Cancer, is certainly more sensitive than you are, but you really will appreciate her thoughtfulness.

Friendly signs for Capricorn: Aries, Cancer, Leo, Sagittarius, Capricorn

star style

No fashion victim are you, Goat girl. Caps are one of the most classic signs—you're confident enough to wear what looks good on you and not just what everyone else has on that season. You're a department store junkie who'd much rather get something with staying power than load up on trendy styles that'll be history by the time the next issue of *W* hits the stands. That's not to say, though, that your wardrobe is boring. No way. You spice up your style with a few key head-turners, like a brightly colored suede jacket or a plaid skirt that's more schoolgirl chic than East Coast prep.

capricorn style sheet

Your best beauty feature: Your slender waist

Look you'll love: A tasteful turtleneck—you'll buy one in every color

Wouldn't be caught dead in: Flashy duds—you have tons of self-confidence and you don't need your clothes to speak for you

Makeup item you can't live without: Eyebrow pencil

Scent pick: Ultra-feminine fragrances that are sweet-smelling, flowery, and a little on the light side

Fashion diva: Kate Moss

matters of the heart

A Capricorn girl is liable to let her shy side come out when it comes time to connect with a guy. But tongue-tied you're not. You're probably just making a few mental notes of this guy's possibilities in the love department...like, will he be as serious as you are about things? Can he ever truly understand you? After all, you're not going to give your heart on a platter to just any guy—he who can't pass the Cap test may not get a cold-hearted rejection, he just won't get any reception at all!

The good news is that when you decide to date someone, you'll be caring, compassionate (though not in an on-fire kinda way), and committed. So long as he doesn't try to make a move in public! Yikes—if a guy could just figure out that you're a private person, he'd have much better luck with you.

Other solid earth signs, like a Taurus, a Virgo, or another Capricorn, seem to really understand you and can crack your Capricorn code enough to get into your head. While an Aries, Leo, or Sagittarius guy may not be able to comprehend you as well, you'll still have good times with these fun-loving guys. Your more conservative side is likely to squelch any serious chance with a flighty Aquarius or Gemini, and beware of some turbulent times with a Libra. Someone as sensitive or artistic as a water sign (Cancer, Scorpio, or Pisces) can help to bring out your well-concealed emotions.

the capricorn guy

Don't expect the Goat to get all mushy and tell you how much he loves you. The conservative Capricorn guy will treat you sweetly and expect that his polite behavior will be enough to show you how much he cares. He will not, with a capital *N*, want to walk around campus holding hands, and not just because his friends will completely harass him. This guy is just a private person—he'll kiss you when the two of you finally get a moment alone.

If you've got a crush on a Cap, you could be waiting for an eternity for him to get up the guts to ask you out. This guy has a shy side that keeps him from warming up to just anyone. Try making friends with him first so he'll feel comfortable enough to open up to you. Once you win his heart, the gentle Goat will be totally dedicated and devoted. And, hey—you may even get him to stop being so serious all the time.

capricorn guy file

Where to spot him: The track

Win his heart by: Helping him with a school project

Great date: Renting an inspiring movie

Major annoyance: Being embarrassed in public

Astro matches: Scorpio, Virgo, Taurus

Capricorn hottie: Ricky Martin

Part Two:

Beyond
Astrology

There's more to getting into who you are than your horo-scope. While astrology may be the oldest and most widely practiced belief, there are other influences on your behavior that can lend yet more clues into the real you, or (as in the case of Feng Shui) help you to manipulate your surroundings to give you the kind of karma you so need. So for more of a read on yourself, read on.

far east astrology

Chinese astrology is based on the belief that you share traits with the animal that represents the year you were born. As the legend goes, Buddha called upon all the animals in the kingdom to attend a meeting, but only twelve attended, from the aggressive rat to the well-mannered boar. Buddha gave each animal a year of its own, and the characteristics associated with the animal were said to be bestowed upon people born during that year.

the chinese calendar

Use the chart below to figure out which animal year you were born in. These dates are based on the Chinese New Year, which begins in February. So, for instance, if you were born in January of 1986, you would be an Ox.

Rat:	1996	1984	1972
Ox:	1997	1985	1973
Tiger:	1998	1986	1974

Rabbit:	1999	1987	1975
Dragon:	2000	1988	1976
Snake:	2001	1989	1977
Horse:	1990	1978	1966
Sheep:	1991	1979	1967
Monkey:	1992	1980	1968
Rooster:	1993	1981	1969
Dog:	1994	1982	1970
Boar:	1995	1983	1971

the rat

The Rat is said to be the first animal that arrived at Buddha's meeting of the species. But the legend also has it that the Rat jumped off the Ox's back in order to get there first. That said, those born in the year of the Rat are known for being aggressive and clever. Rats also have a huge pack of friends—though an inability to reveal their inner critter leaves them with more acquaintances than true friends.

Curiosity may have killed the cat, but it has made the Rat a very sage, wise sign—the kind who likes to take on any new challenge and try just about anything. Hoarders by nature, Rats like to keep all their stuff neat and organized…and if you've indexed your accessories to keep 'em in order, you are definitely letting the Rat in you come out! Rats are also super-devoted to people in their inner circle, like friends and family. Just try to betray a Rat-packer and you'll get a dose of this rodent's temper.

the ox

No bull about it—the Ox is the strong and solid type. Oxen are goal-oriented and work hard to ensure that they are doing a good job. Friends may harass their Ox-like pal for being a bit on the serious side. Yeah, so you're a little hard-core. But just who do your buds come running to when they get into major trouble? Yup, that's right. The Ox.

Looking at life so seriously, Oxen sometimes feel left out of the party and maybe even a little lonely. If only they knew how much people admired them. With qualities like faithfulness, honesty, and integrity, it's no wonder an Ox is so admirable.

the tiger

Cool cats that they are, Tigers have magnetic personalities that draw people to them. On the one hand, the Tiger can be gentle and affectionate, the kind of person friends want to tell their deepest secrets to and the kind of girl guys want to cuddle with. Almost no one can resist this adorable animal...when it's in a good mood. But fire up the Tiger's temper and you're in for one big catfight. Tigers are also known for being confident, courageous, and quick to drop cash. Shopping sprees are a definite Tiger specialty.

the rabbit

Everybody wants to have a Rabbit around. Cute and friendly, the Rabbit rarely lets anything get her down. And no matter how much she messes up, no one has the heart to break bad news to this bunny. (Thankfully, her multiple friends will steer her clear of any trouble.)

Check out a Rabbit's closet and you'll find clothes galore. A real style-setter, she can do bohemian just as easily as she can do preppy.

the dragon

Dragons are one of the most gifted signs in the Chinese zodiac. They're the stars of the animal years. Powerful and intelligent, a Dragon is a natural-born leader. Seeking that committee spot on your school's activity board, Dragon girl? Go for it. Better yet, run for student body prez!

Dragon dames are also rarely dateless. But will any guy match up to your high expectations? Hmmm...even Freddie Prinze Jr. might have trouble slaying your picky side.

the snake

Snakes like being the center of attention, and their stories tend to get bigger as their audience size grows. A Snake's charming nature attracts both friends and crushes...but she can get oh-so-jealous when her buds and boyfriends don't give her the time of day.

The Snake sign is also associated with cash. There won't be any worrying about the green stuff for the Snake girl—she's got a big-enough stash to put a down payment on that cherry-red Cabrio.

the horse

Very little can keep a Horse girl locked up in her stable for long—her need to get out and see the world is far too strong. Horses are energetic and often impatient. They'll blow a lame party before giving it a chance to pick up and head to where they hear the action is.

At the heart of the Horse, though, is someone who is somewhat inse-cure, searching high and low to fit in. Contradictory to her behavior? You bet. But the Horse is the poster animal for contradiction—independent yet seeking that someone special, proud yet modest, sweet-natured yet hot-blooded. No wonder she feels pulled in different directions!

the sheep

The Sheep is charming, creative, and artistic. This gentle creature is driven by the need to feel loved and admired, and the slightest bit of conflict can send a Sheep over the edge. She's so well mannered that she's as liked by her friends' parents as she is by her friends.

The best way for a Sheep girl to show off her talents is through her creativity. She'll send her boyfriend off on a scavenger hunt to find his birthday gift, and she'll write a poem especially for a pal. Just don't expect the Sheep to be too organized and detail-oriented. Appearances are also a top priority for the Sheep. Pity the brother or sister who has to share a room with the Sheep!

the monkey

Monkeys are out to have a good time, and they win over others with their charm and wit. As opposed to hanging with just one clique, the Monkey prefers to get in on the action with all kinds of different crews. At lunch, you can find her hobnobbing with the computer whiz kids before heading over to talk sports with the jocks. Not only does this help quell the Monkey's insatiable curiosity, it also makes her knowledgeable on many different subjects.

Monkeys have a tendency to look out for themselves at the expense of friends' feelings. But on the flip side of this, when you have a problem, there's no better bud than a Monkey to help solve things.

the rooster

Roosters are perceptive and quick—they don't let anything get by them. A Rooster girl will guess who you're crushing on before you even e-mail her about it. With a Rooster, what you see is what you get. She's not into covering up what she thinks or hiding behind a façade just to fit in.

What she is into, though, is fashion. Roosters are best-dressed at any function, and they know how to put together a stylish wardrobe on a student's budget. Roosters also have trouble sitting still. Rarely will a Rooster be holed up in her bedroom.

the dog

Just like the four-legged type, Dogs are loyal and faithful. They'll stand by their friends in the worst of times and defend them to the end. If you tell a Dog your most-guarded secrets, she'll bury them deep in her soul and never reveal a thing. But a Dog girl may not find it so easy to open up her heart and spill all; it takes this cautious critter a little longer than most to open up to others.

Moodiness can bring a Dog girl down, and she conceals inner feelings with a powerful bark that keeps people away until she's ready to deal with them.

the boar

The Boar (which is a male pig) is the perfectionist of the Chinese zodiac, from looks to manners. In fact, the Boar was probably the last animal to Buddha's party because it was making sure it looked just right. But even though they set super-high standards for themselves, Boars are not prone to being overly judgmental of others. Quite the contrary. Boars have a huge heart—they see the good in others and strive to please people. There's nothing more satisfying to a Boar girl than putting a smile on a pal's face. Boars are also extremely intelligent and are always on a knowledge quest.

it's a numbers game

Just as Chinese astrology associates people with animals for cosmic clues, numerology assigns people with numbers in order to gain added insight. The father of numerology is Pythagoras, the Greek mathematician. The basic concept is that numbers hold related cosmic vibrations and the sum of things—like your birth date or complete name—hold numeric values that you can read into. If all of this numbers stuff is confusing you more than a math test, don't fret. It's easy to figure out your numbers, and even easier to read about what your numbers mean.

destiny calls

Your destiny number is the one that offers the most info on your life. It's the key to your inner core—why you do what you do and act the way you act.

You can calculate your destiny number by adding the month, day, and year of your birthday together and then reducing it to a single digit. Say your birthday is January 10, 1985, or 1/10/1985. You'd get to a number between one and nine by doing the following:

Step One: $1+10+1985=1996$

Step Two: $1+9+9+6=25$

Step Three: $2+5=7$

Destiny Number for 1/10/1985 is 7

Once you determine your number, take a look at the following pages to see what it's all about.

We're Number One! We're Number One! Ones wanna win, that's for sure. The most competitive of the destiny digits, you won't even get in the game unless you know you have a chance of winning. Ones are also independent thinkers— you'd rather do things your way and mess up than try the same old, same old and get the same old results.

A One needs "me time" like no other number, and you may feel the need to shut everyone out of your world while you're in your zone. But once you come out, you can turn on the charm and make everyone pretty much forget you just blew them off.

On the friendship front, Ones make connections with other unique souls, but if their personalities are too strong, watch out— your need to be number one will make this a battle to be leader.

Careers in your destiny: lawyer, business manager, inventor, artist

#2

Peace-loving Twos want nothing more than for everyone to get along. You believe strongly in sisterhood and would no sooner betray a best friend than you would shave off all your hair (way too bold a move for most Twos, by the way). A Two can be overly sensitive at times, especially when your basic belief that all people are good gets blown to pieces. One way to bring you out of the blues is by listening to all kinds of music.

A Two can find fun in most any activity, so even if your friends drag you to yet another boy band concert, you'll find yourself singing along with the boys before the night is through. Twos are also good listeners, which is probably why your phone rings at all hours with friends needing advice on the other end of the line.

Careers in your destiny: psychologist, writer, dancer, musician

#3

Threes are pumped up on life—full of energy and ready for a new adventure almost anytime. They're attracted to the arts and to sports, both watching and participating.

Some Threes are complete slobs on the home front—piles of clothes and books everywhere in your room and just a big enough pathway to get from the bed to the closet. Others of you are the complete opposite—neat freaks who freak out when someone messes with their stuff.

You choose your confidantes carefully, preferring girls who are upbeat and fun to be around. Without even wanting to be part of the school social scene, you and your fun group of friends can't help but be popular.

Careers in your destiny: teacher, photographer, journalist, physical therapist

#4

Fours get satisfaction out of a job well done and are as hard-working as numbers come. There's nothing better for a Four than to tackle a huge school project and get the great grade to go along with it. As a Four, you probably already have a few career choices picked out and are hoping this whole school thing won't take too long—you're anxious to dive into the real world. Behind any budding entrepreneur—the girl you know selling her cute handmade handbags or the high school's computer whiz making a mint designing Web sites—you'll probably find the number four somewhere in her charts.

Fours value responsibility in their friends and have a hard time handling flakes. They can also be quite the magazine junkies; you probably have subscriptions to more than one fashion mag.

Careers in your destiny: designer, fashion buyer, entrepreneur, salesperson

#5

Restless Fives get bored easily. Your wardrobe is ever changing, as you fall for trends every season when designers come out with new styles. You also tend to have a ton of hobbies and interests. You look forward to new school years and the start of class, but before too long you're wondering when you can sign on for a new subject.

You don't go through friends fast. Instead, your adventuresome attitude draws like-minded girls, and together you get in on all the action you can find. Guys are attracted to your wild side, and some are drawn to the challenge of trying to tame you…a task that will end in failure for them. For a fun-loving Five, life is truly a party.

Careers in your destiny: marketing manager, magazine editor, interpreter, pilot

#6

How do you spot a Six at a party? Simple—she's usually the one throwing it, or at least helping out. Sixes can't help but be responsible—you probably started baby-sitting before you were even 10. Friends in need find that a Six will not only lend a shoulder to cry on, but also offer practical advice to get them through the sitch unscathed.

Sixes also love to give. In fact, you're probably involved in more than one volunteer organization. Sixes tend to get wrapped up in matters of the heart. Like everything else in life, you try to be logical about love. But like anyone who falls for the wrong guy all the time can tell you—there's no logic to love.

Careers in your destiny: veterinarian, doctor, social worker, party planner, professor

#7

Sevens can seem a little shy to those who don't know them. But while they may look like they're being wallflowers at social events, they're probably just getting a good read on the place and observing what's going on around them before diving into the action.

On a constant quest for information, you're one of the most intellectual numbers. You also have a knack for getting your girlfriends to reveal everything to you—but secrets are always safe with a Seven.

Sevens need an environment that's out of the ordinary, so your room just has to show some signs of creative life. Ditto your wardrobe. While you may get your clothes in the same stores as all your friends, no doubt you make yours unique with things like cool accessories.

Careers in your destiny: computer programmer, writer, scientist, graphic designer

#8

In an Eight's world, friends and family come first. You're a people-person, that's for sure, but you're choosy about which people you want to get personal with. Not in a snobby way, though—you are so against anything or anyone that reeks of snobbery.

Unless you're loaded with cash, you'd better seriously consider getting a part-time job. Eights like to have the best. You choose quality over quantity, so even though you may not have as many clothes in your closet as all your friends, your stuff is sweet.

Another Eight trait is your great taste. (How many times has a friend called you for clothes suggestions before a big party?) Your friends can't help but have crushes on the guys you go out with.

Careers in your destiny: interior designer, stockbroker, sales-person, real estate developer

#9

As a Nine, you have a strong desire—OK, a major need—to be appreciated and recognized. You're also a master when it comes to standing out in a crowd. Smart, sophisticated, and socially gift-ed, you can work a room better than Oprah.

A little on the artsy side, you gravitate toward activities like drama, painting, and writing poetry. You're attracted to the kind of guy who isn't afraid to show some emotion. If he can't let you know how much you mean to him, he'll be looking for a new date in no time.

What's coolest about a Nine, though, is how much of a giver you are. You'd gladly give up your spare time to volunteer for a wor-thy cause, even if it's helping a friend repaint her room. No problem is too huge for you to take on, dear Nine.

Careers in your destiny: politician, therapist, actor, artist

getting an attitude

Wondering why you do the things you do? Your attitude number might lend some insight. This number represents the attitude you exhibit to others—how and why you act the way you do. To get your attitude number, you need to add the month you were born to the day you were born. For instance, if your birthday is March 7 (3/7), you'd do the following:

Step One: $3+7=10$

Step Two: $1+0=1$

The attitude number for a March 7 birthday is 1. (Note: If you added the numbers together and got a single digit, use that as your attitude number.)

Here's what it means.

#1

A One possesses a strong dose of astro energy. With confidence galore, your personal power puts you at the lead in any situation. You like to have your way—a quality that can cause some parental conflict when they fail to see things your way. You're also bold and courageous—leave it to a One to tell a teacher you think she's being unfair.

#2

Twos are eternal peacemakers. If your friends are having a fight, you will somehow manage to hep them get over it and move on. Nothing bothers you more than conflict, and you try to avoid having it in your life. Twos are also total team players, and not just when it comes to sports. So long as it's good for the group, it's good for you. And because you're so on the ball, you're given a lot of responsibility. (Maybe that's why you're stuck baby-sitting your little brother on a Saturday night!)

#3

Threes are master communicators. You know how to rally your group of friends for an impromptu get-together at your place. (After, of course, you've smooth-talked your parents into letting you throw it.) You also have clever ways of getting out of things you don't want to do, like the chores you just talked your sister into doing in exchange for letting her borrow your suede pants. You also have an incredible amount of energy, making you fun to be around and hard to keep up with!

#4

Ah, the industrious Four. No slacker are you; Fours thrive on working hard. You're dedicated to every project you take on—the homecoming float you design makes the others look like flops.

The friends you attract aren't exactly rule-breakers, which is a lot like you...most of the time. Every now and then, though, you get the urge to do something completely out of the ordinary and a little on the edge. Thankfully, those cautious pals will reel you in before you get into trouble.

#5

Fives surround themselves with people from varied backgrounds and cultures. Someone just like you would bore you...not because you're boring (oh, no!), but because you wouldn't learn anything new from her.

A Five is alive with energy, and you constantly have to be doing something. You tend to get bored with long projects or books and movies that seem to go on endlessly. (Admit it, you've been ready to bolt from the movie theater on more than one occasion.) To a Five, change is good.

#6

Sixes are the humanitarians of the numerology world—and are always willing to take on a worthy cause. Most of the time, you're pretty mellow—until, that is, someone offends your values or ethics.

Without even having to try too hard, you're great in school. You're responsible and conscientious, always getting homework done and paying close attention in class. When friends try to talk during a class or pass you a note, you flash them a "get real" look that indicates it's not the time or place to socialize.

#7

Sevens have a great (though sometimes a little twisted) sense of humor, thanks to a vivid imagination and creativity you've yet to fully unleash. The Seven has the mark of genius behind it, but as it is with every Einstein, geniuses can sometimes be misunderstood. Hard as it may be at a time in your life when fitting in is everything, don't be afraid to stand out.

Sevens tend to express themselves through the arts. Writing, poetry, painting, and drama are all good ways to express your innovative ideas.

#8

The number Eight rules money and fame. Not that you necessarily have either one at the moment, but you definitely dream about getting your hands on the green stuff. Eights like to take the lead in situations, but they can also fall in line and do what's expected of them. You have a basic desire to play by the rules, and you like your friends to do the same.

At the heart of an Eight, though, is someone who wants to be somebody—you're just trying to figure out if that's best done by following the rules or taking the reins.

#9

The noble Nine has a taste for the finer things in life. Your class and style show through in every aspect of your life. You have a fairly easygoing attitude and don't rock the boat unless majorly provoked. (A Nine temper, though in hiding most of the time, can be fierce.) You're not as assertive as you should be in all areas of your life, and you may do things you know aren't the best for you just because you find it hard to take a stand. At the same time, your Nine attitude makes you exceptionally talented and a great student.

palm piloting

You're holding a few secrets to life in the palm of your hand. That maze of lines crisscrossing your pad holds clues to who you are—it's like a road map to your past, present, and future. To get a grip on yours, first figure out which hand holds your destiny. For a basic palm reading, you read the dominant hand—the right if you're right-handed and vice versa.

the shape of things to come

Is your hand square or oblong? Figure out the shape of your palm to determine if your head is in the clouds or if your feet are firmly planted on the ground.

oblong hand

If you're long on palm, you've got a vivid imagination and can pass the time in any boring class by daydreaming. You're a master at coming up with good ideas—the perfect antidote to friends who are content with spending every Saturday night at the movies.

square hand

You're a pretty practical person who relies on facts—not those oh-so-unpredictable emotions—to make decisions. But while you're down-to-earth, you're not down on energy. Your enthusiasm puts you on the A-list of party invites.

heart line

head line

fame line

life line

Get the long and short of your personality by honing in on whether your fingers are long or short.

short fingers

If your digits are on the diminutive side, you're on a perpetual quest to have a good time. If something (or someone) can't keep you entertained, it's history. (C'mon, admit it—you're a chronic channel surfer.) You also know how to juggle several projects at once.

long fingers

Fingers a little lengthy? You like to look at things in careful detail and are known for being extremely patient. Maybe that's why your friends send you to stand in line eight hours for Limp Bizkit tickets. You understand every little hidden nuance, making it tough for anyone to slip a fast one by you.

thumb tracking

Can you contort your thumb in unnatural positions? If your thumb is flexible—meaning it can bend backward from the joint—you like to kick back and keep things conflict-free. If your thumb is firm and won't budge backward at all, you're determined, reliable, and maybe just a tad stubborn.

heart line

Where it is: It runs under the padded areas just below your fingers.

What it means: Not only are your past, present, and potential boyfriends buried in this line, it also holds clues to your emotions and how willing you are to give. The section of the line that's nearest your index finger is what is happening or has happened in your youth...farther along toward your pinkie shows what's in store. And the little lines that branch up from your heart line reveal the romances in your future. If your line is long and curved, you have a pleasant, romantic nature. A short line could mean either you don't get overly gushy about affairs of the heart, or your one true love will be so deep and strong that it makes everything else in your love life pale in comparison. Don't worry that you're destined to be dateless if your love line is barely visible—it most likely just shows that you're more logical than emotional when it comes to matters of the heart.

head line

Where it is: It runs from the top of your life line through the center of the palm.

What it means: The head line is logic central. It conveys just how you use your brainpower to navigate your way through life. A long head line is said to be a sign of a strong, by-the-books intellect. You've got the potential to amaze your teachers. The longer the head line is, the more complex and involved your thinking tends to be. You may give things way too much thought. (If it looks like a rose and smells like a rose, just call it a rose, okay?) A line that curves downward is a clue that you're creative, while a straight line means you're both creative and analytical. Got a squatty line that curves upward? You may be scattered in your thinking and on the forgetful side. No clear logic line? Hmmm...let's just say emotions rule your every move.

life line

Where it is: It runs around the base of your thumb.

What it means: Before you panic 'cause your life line is soooo short, take note: The life line does not—repeat, *not*—reveal how long you will live. It's more of a measure of your energy and enthusiasm toward life and gives a clue as to how you react when you're completely stressed. The longer your life line, the more energetic you are. A shorter life line is a clue that you're more mellow. And a thin, wavy line means that when life starts to get insane on you, downtime does you good. Long hot bath, anyone?

fame line

Where it is: It runs from the center of your wrist toward your middle finger.

What it means: Cindy Crawford-status is not guaranteed by a long fame line. This palm imprint is merely an indication of what you're capable of achieving and your attitude toward success. The longer your fame line, the more likely it is you'll achieve your dreams. The farther down your palm it goes, the earlier in life you'll grab hold of those goals. But don't take a number in the loser line if you can't spot a solid line down the center of your palm—no significant fame line can mean that your life will be filled with so many different things that you won't wind up going down one specific path.

zen and the art of cleaning your room

Love life a drag? Grades on a downward slump? Could be your bedroom's to blame, so says the ancient practice of Feng Shui. According to this 4,000-year-old Chinese art, the vibes that your surroundings set off can affect everything from your love life to your mood to your health. The basic idea is that every little detail in your room's decor—from the location of your bed to that pile of dirty clothes building up in one corner of the room—can either work for you or create some majorly bad karma. But fear not. You can put your life on a more positive path with an easy room redo or by incorporating Feng Shui design elements in your life. Read on for a primer on the principles of Feng Shui.

chi me

If you want to get on the good-vibes express, you'll need to introduce some positive energy flow into your world. In Feng Shui, it's called "chi" energy and it flows through everything, including your body. If you've got good chi going through you, other people can sometimes sense those positive vibes and you'll attract winners into your world. Likewise, the flow of bad chi through you sets negative vibes, basically inviting bad karma your way. Luckily, chi energy can be manipulated by how you feel and by your surroundings. Make your room a positive-energy palace and good chi will flow through. Hang out with friends who are easygoing and have a sense of humor, and you, too, will feel the good vibes. Study in a schoolroom that seems to suck the life out of you and you'll feel the brain drain; move to an area that's energizing and watch those answers pour onto the pages in front of you. By getting a feel for the chi energy within you and around you, you can tap into its positive power and steer clear from its unfavorable energy.

yin, yang, and you

There are two kinds of energy in the Feng Shui world, yin—passive energy—and yang—active energy. Yin is the side of you that's creative and sensitive. Yang is the side of you that's social and energetic. Each of us has both yin and yang energy, though some have more of one than the other. (Witness your lazy brother sleeping on the couch who harbors way too much yin.) You can use yin and yang to your advantage by learning to balance both in yourself, your surroundings, and situations with other people.

To get the balance right, you first have to figure out whether you are too yin or too yang. If you're feeling a little lethargic and unmotivated, your yin could use a little yang infusion. On the other hand, if you're aggressive and impatient, you need to introduce some yin into your world. Check out the charts on the next page for tips on balancing your energy.

yin influences	Sports	Foods	Activities	Colors
	Yoga Swimming Meditation Stretching	Ice cream Sweet snacks Tofu Fruit Salads	Listening to music Watching TV Reading Talking on the phone Sleeping	Blue Green
yang influences	Sports	Foods	Activities	Colors
	Karate Aerobics Tennis Running	Meat Eggs Salty snacks Whole-grain breads	Playing games Studying Surfing the Internet Going out with friends	Red Orange

the chi compass

According to the principles of Feng Shui, there are eight different types of chi energy, which are associated with eight different directions. The direction of your room itself, as well as where you place things inside your room, are all affected by the chi energy of a particular direction. So while your desk may look pretty cool under your window, if it's facing the wrong direction chi-wise, your study habits could be seriously compromised. Take a look at the following chart to get the scoop on the different types of chi energy.

North: This direction represents beginnings, growth, and learning. It has a quiet and calm energy and stimulates independence from others and even a sense of isolation.

Northeast: Energy is strong here—think competitiveness and a desire to show your strength and assert your individuality. Move your desk here for some major brain surges.

East: This one's an ambitious direction that's also associated with helping those close to you and staying focused on things. Pictures of friends and family placed here will ensure that they're never far from your thoughts.

Southeast: This direction represents maturity and the forming of romantic relationships. Got love letters to stash or a journal to record your deepest thoughts in? Head for the southeast corner of your pad.

South: In this direction, public recognition and success are yours. It represents brilliance and social success. If your phone never seems to ring, try moving it to the southern section of your room.

Southwest: This could prove to be the homiest spot in your room, where you feel a sense of harmony and calm.

West: After a long day of school and activities, retreat to the west for a little R&R. Got something you want to read? Plop yourself in this direction for concentration galore.

Northwest: The energy here is associated with organization and leadership, and maybe even sharing some of your infinite wisdom with others. You're at your wisest when in this area.

rearranging your life

Using the principles of Feng Shui and the concept of chi energy, you can turn your room into a temple of good vibes. Before you get started on the room redo, you'll need to know which direction your house and your room face. It's easily figured out with a map of the neighborhood or by using that old compass you got in Girl Scouts that you thought you'd never have another use for. Get the gist of which way your house is facing, then draw a simple diagram of your room's four walls, pointing out which wall is located in the north, south, east, and west.

where your bed heads

The direction you sleep in has an effect on how well you'll catch your zzz's and how life will look when you're awake. Use this chart to figure out what kind of karma your sleeping space has on you now, and where you can move your bed to make the changes you crave.

Pillow to the North: This spot will make it simple for you to sleep soundly (though it may make you a little too tranquil after you've woken up). Another plus for this position: It'll help increase your spirituality and put you at peace with just about everyone.

Pillow to the Northeast: Feng Shui masters advise against keeping your bed in this direction for too long a time. While it will get your energy up, it may make it tough to ever get a good, peaceful night's sleep.

Pillow to the East: Life looks good when your head points to the east. It gives you just the right dose of optimism needed to make you motivated and ambitious, but not too much energy to zap you of much-needed zzz's.

Pillow to the Southeast: If you want to tap into your creative potential, try sleeping with your head pointed in this direction. It's also an ideal spot to snooze if you want to improve your communications skills.

Pillow to the South: Feeling a little fiery lately? Could be it's because you're sleeping in a direction that revs up your emotions and energies. So if you find yourself ready to snap at someone again, maybe you should consider moving your bed.

Pillow to the Southwest: If you're experiencing some parental probs or fights with friends, try switching your bed to this position to increase the peace. The only problem with the most harmonious of spots to sleep? You may start becoming too dependent on others.

Pillow to the West: Good sleep and a great atmosphere await you when you move your bed and point your head to the west. It can also help you in the love area of your life. Just don't let all this contentment make you unmotivated.

Pillow to the Northwest: You rule! With your head pointed northwest, you let you inner bossy-girl come out. Being so in control, too, you find it easy to get a good night's sleep.

inviting in good karma

Are you letting bad vibes into your bedroom? If your door is in the wrong place, you just might be welcoming the wrong kind of karma into your space. Check out this chart to find out how to fix any Feng Shui faux paus.

Direction of Your Door	Chi Energy	Solution
North	Peace and quiet (meaning, no visitors)	Add a little red by putting a poster on the door or painting the door (clear it with your folks first), and you'll add much-needed energy.

Direction of Your Door	Chi Energy	Solution
Northwest	Represents organization and control and always being on the ball	If you feel the need to mellow out a bit, put a plant in a metallic container near the door.
West	Romance could come your way, but so could laziness.	Something metal will rev up your mood, so put a picture in a metal frame nearby.
Southwest	Instability and restlessness	Increase the peace with a bowl of sea salt placed near the door.
South	Major activity, action, and occasional arguments	Calm things down with a color like blue, green, purple, or even black. If painting the door isn't an option, accessorize the entrance area with frames, candles, or decorative vases in these colors.
Southeast	Great for communication and peace	Play up this perfect location with wood accessories or furniture near the door, plus shades of blue and green.

East	Promotes growth and learning even more	The colors green and off-white will increase the good chi energy.
Northeast	Causes excitability and occasional irritation	Correct your chi with a bright white door and shiny metal fixtures to reflect negative energy away from your room.

best for the bedroom

If you want that positive chi energy to flow, follow some of these Feng Shui bedroom basics.

Stash that trash: All that clutter that fills your room can just zap the karma right out of the place. Put things in their places—throw your clothes in the laundry, recycle the stacks of magazines you've been collecting since the sixth grade, trash the mascara that's turned into one big clump, and find a happy home for those stuffed animals your ex won for you at the state fair. Or at least keep the clutter hidden in the closet.

Out with shabby sheets: Sure, those Snow White sheets in 100 percent polyester have special meaning to you, but they're turning your room into a Feng Shui faux pas. Do yourself a favor: Ditch the patterns. Ditto the synthetic materials. Then get yourself a set of cotton, linen, or silk sheets in a calming color, like soft white or a pastel, and remake your bed.

Liven up your space: Adding live plants to your room can work wonders on your life. Get ones with soft, rounded edges, place them in the west or northwest part of the room, and don't forget to water them.

Deck the walls: The right artwork on your walls can work chi wonders. Get art that suits your style. Bright-colored art can stimulate your mind, while soft colors can be soothing and peaceful. Mirrors reflect energy right back atcha, trapping all the emotion you feel inside of you. Keep them in the bathroom or in the closet so you can get a good night's sleep.

Add a coat of karmic color: Pastels are the most peaceful wall colors for your room, so if you want a room that's restful, that shade of ballerina pink just might do the job. Colors like red or burgundy will increase the energy, while deeper blues and greens will add an earthy energy to the place.

Here's a look at some colorful choices to consider:

Brown: Added as an accent color, this hue will add stability and help you concentrate.

Taupe: Give your walls this tone when you want to feel safe, secure, and snuggly.

Peach: Warm, with just a hint of energy, this shade provides a perfect balance of yin and yang.

Orange: This deep hue can add a calm brightness to a dark and gloomy room.

Bright yellow: This sunny shade adds a bit of energy while maintaining an overall warmth.

Lime green: This bright color adds new life and optimism to your atmosphere while offering a sense of stability.

Emerald green: Like the color in nature, this shade represents tree energy and adds excitement without overdoing it.

Blue: A deep shade of a blue hue can add a sense of calm to a room that's too bright.

Blue-green: By mixing peaceful blue with deep-thinking green, you'll introduce both relaxation and creativity.

Light blue: If your room is a place you want to relax only, paint it this soothing color (and plan on doing your homework elsewhere!).

Lavender: Unlike fiery purple, this softer shade is stimulating without being overbearing and creates the perfect place for socializing and hanging out.

Pink: Not surprisingly, this color will let you bring out your playful, young side.

objects of desire

Not everyone can rearrange things in her room to make the world a little brighter. You may have a closet-sized space that makes moving the bed into anywhere but the hallway impossible, or you could have a roommate who suddenly decides she's claiming the side of the room you were about to take over. No problem! You can load up on objects that bring in good vibes, like the ones below. Just consider this your personal Feng Shui shopper.

Crystals: When sunlight passes through them, cut-glass crystals send all different colors of light beaming out in different directions. This is good for sending sparks of chi energy your way.

Candles: Candles are the objects of romance and passion. Gaze into the flame to rev up your creativity, or place two candles together to try and get a relationship going. Tall candles are better for channeling chi energy than squatty ones, and white or light-colored candles beat dark-colored candles on the chi scale. Candles are good, but house fires are very bad—blow those babies out before you leave the room or fall asleep.

Water: Water can bring in new chi energy that's good for your overall outlook. Placed in the east or southeast part of your room, it can rev up your social life or love life by sending in good chi energy. If a fish tank isn't your thing, get an indoor mini-fountain and let the fresh energy flow.

Clocks: Is your life in complete chaos? The rhythmic ticking of a clock (so very yang-like) can introduce order into your life. A digital clock defeats the purpose here, so get a ticker if you can.

Conclusion

By now, your mind may be spinning with insight into the inner you. And you may need to take another peek at the pages to get a grasp of what you're all about and why you do the things you do. Hopefully, though, the astro info provided in this book has given you a greater understanding of yourself and of the other people in your world.

Remember, too, that beyond astrology, Chinese astrology, and every other form of cosmic charting are environmental influences. Where you're raised, how you're raised, and who you hang around with shape who you are, too. So just 'cause you're supposed to be one way according to your sign or your number doesn't mean that you don't act another way. And willpower can be stronger than any planetary influence—so you're free to change any cosmic quality that you can't stand. What you've discovered in this book should, though, start you on a path toward self-discovery and give you tools to continue figuring out who you are.